WOOD WORKING
FOR
BEGINNERS

WOOD
WORKING
FOR
BEGINNERS

Albert Jackson & David Day

The Lyons Press
Guilford, Connecticut
An imprint of The Globe Pequot Press

First Lyons Press edition, 2001

**First published in 1998
by HarperCollins Publishers, London**

Copyright © HarperCollins Publishers, 1998

The Lyons Press is an imprint of The Globe Pequot Press.

Printed in Singapore

10 9 8 7 6 5 4 3 2 1

Cover design: Simon Jennings
Cover photograph: Ben Jennings

The Library of Congress Cataloging-in-Print Data is available on file.

ISBN 1 58574-426-3

ACKNOWLEDGMENTS

Reference material and equipment
*The authors and producers are grateful to the
following for supplying reference, materials and
equipment used in this book:*

John Boddy's Fine Wood & Tool Store Ltd.,
Boroughbridge, Yorkshire, UK
Robert Bosch Ltd., Uxbridge, Middlesex, UK
Buck & Hickman Ltd., Sheffield, S. Yorkshire, UK
C.F. Anderson & Sons Ltd., London, N1, UK
CSM Trade Supplies, Brighton, East Sussex, UK
Elu Power Tools Ltd., Slough, Berkshire, UK
Emmerich (Berlon) Ltd., Ashford, Kent, UK
FIDOR, Feltham, Middlesex, UK
Foxell & James, London, EC1, UK
Garrett Wade, New York, NY, USA
Langlows Products Division, Palace Chemicals Ltd.,
Chesham, Bucks, UK
Libron, New Romney, Kent, UK
Record Marples Ltd., Sheffield, S. Yorkshire, UK
Robert Sorby Ltd., Sheffield, S. Yorkshire, UK
Ronseal Ltd., Chapeltown, Sheffield, UK
Rustins Ltd., London, NW2, UK
The Stanley Works Ltd., Sheffield, S. Yorkshire, UK
Tilgear Ltd., Cuffley, Hertfordshire, UK

Photography
*The studio photographs for this book were taken by
Neil Waving, with the following exceptions:*

Ben Jennings, pages 77, 98, 99, 100, 101, 106, 110,
112, 114, 122.

*The authors and producers also acknowledge
additional photography by, and the use of
photographs from, the following:*

Robert Bosch Ltd., Uxbridge, Middlesex, UK, page
105. *Council of Forest Industries Canada,* West
Byfleet, Surrey, UK, page 52. *Cuprinol Ltd.,* Frome,
Somerset, UK, page 116. *Karl Danzer,* Maldon,
Essex, UK, page 51. *John Hunnex,* Woodchurch,
Kent, UK, page 58(T), 121(CL) *International Festival
of the Sea (Peter Chesworth),* Bristol, UK, page 58(B).
Gavin Jordan, Buckinghamshire College, High
Wycombe, Bucks, UK, page 48. *Langlows Products
Division – Palace Chemicals Ltd.,* Chesham, Bucks,
UK, page 124. *Georg Ott Werkzeug-Und Maschinen
Fabric GMBH & Co.,* Germany, page 11. *Stewart
Linford Furniture,* High Wycombe, Bucks, UK, (*Theo
Bergstrom*), page 59, (*Derek St Romain*), page 120.
Ronseal Ltd., Chapeltown, Sheffield, UK, page
121(TR). *Simo Hannelius,* Helsinki, Finland, page 60.
Richard Williams, Buckinghamshire College, High
Wycombe, Bucks, UK, page 121(BR).

Key to credits
T = top, B = bottom, L = left, R = right, TL = top left,
TC = top center, TR = top right, CL = center left, C = center,
CR = center right, BL = bottom left, BC = bottom center,
BR = bottom right.

CONTENTS

Introduction

Woodworking encompasses a great many diverse activities, including turning, woodcarving, marquetry, cabinetmaking, and joinery, but every specialist craftsman or craftswoman has at some time mastered the fundamentals of measuring and marking, dimensioning, assembling, and finishing—the basic woodworking skills that are at the core of this book.

Marking out the wood for a project requires an ability to think in three dimensions, and to imagine how one component fits with another and in what order. You also need to know which tools are going to give the best results, depending on the level of accuracy required and the properties of the wood you are using.

Dimensioning is the process of reducing raw materials accurately to size. This almost invariably entails planing components square and true—a procedure that is simple in principle but takes practice to perfect.

All but the simplest of woodworking projects involve cutting and assembling a variety of joints. Jointmaking has long been regarded as a measure of a woodworker's skills, because to make a good joint you need not only expert hand-and-eye coordination, but the experience that tells you the best way to fasten one piece of wood to another attractively and discreetly without sacrificing strength.

The finishing of wood is so important to a project's appearance that traditionally it was regarded as a separate trade skill. It may be the application of a varnish or polish that brings out the true color and beauty of the wood, but the key to successful results is careful preparation of the surface—a somewhat tedious but vital part of the job.

One necessary adjunct to these pivotal skills is an appreciation of how wood behaves. It is a unique, living material that continues to swell and contract with changes in humidity, a factor that a woodworker must deal with in the design and construction of every project. You will discover that some woods are easier to work than others—and that each piece, regardless of species, is unique in the way the grain twists and turns. This is one reason why we have chosen to concentrate almost exclusively on the use of hand tools. There is a valid argument for suggesting that woodwork is easier, faster, and potentially more accurate using power tools or machines, but working with hand tools is the surest way to develop the knack of cutting and shaping wood without tearing the grain. Moreover, as every experienced woodworker will tell you, you can often complete a task with hand tools in less time than it takes to set up the relevant machinery. There is a place for mechanized tools in every workshop—but because they are relatively expensive, it makes sense to wait until you know from experience what you enjoy doing most, so you can equip yourself with the most appropriate machines.

Woodworking is a fascinating and rewarding pastime, but it would be misleading to imply that it is easy or to suggest that a book is instantly going to turn you into a competent craftsperson. Practical experience is by far the most effective teacher, and all any book can hope to do is cajole, encourage, and guide you in the right direction, so you have more chance of picking up good habits rather than bad ones, and to provide you with a sound foundation upon which you can build.

SETTING UP A WORKSHOP

It is difficult to do decent work without a safe and well-organized workshop. Perhaps you could convert a spare room or garage into a small workshop, particularly if you plan to use the minimum of hand tools. But dust, fumes, and noise may be a nuisance, and you need plenty of room if you want to do anything other than small-scale woodwork. Where possible, make use of an outbuilding, such as a garage. Being relatively large, garage doors provide easy access for raw materials, and you've probably got light and power already installed. Alternatively, use a reasonably large wood-frame garden shed, but insulate it to create comfortable working conditions and a stable environment for the wood. The insulant can be concealed behind man-made-board panels, which will serve as backing for tool storage and for wall racks and shelves to keep your materials in good order.

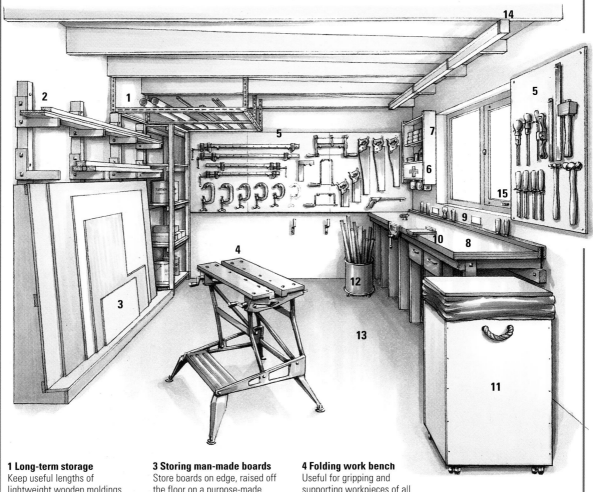

1 Long-term storage
Keep useful lengths of lightweight wooden moldings and similar materials on a suspended metal-angle rack.

2 Storing wood
Where practicable, store larger sections of wood on strong wall-mounted brackets bolted securely to the wall. Do not overload them.

3 Storing man-made boards
Store boards on edge, raised off the floor on a purpose-made frame that provides good support and prevents the panels from distorting. Place smaller boards at the front.

4 Folding work bench
Useful for gripping and supporting workpieces of all shapes and sizes, a folding work bench can be employed for jobs around the house as well as in the workshop. When not in use, the folded bench can be stored on wall-mounted brackets.

Equipping a workshop

The workshop opposite is designed for a small garage or large garden shed. If the width of your workspace does not allow a large fitted bench along one side, as shown, build one against the shorter end wall or use a freestanding cabinetmaker's bench. Even if you don't have an extensive selection of tools now, allow ample storage space for additional tools and equipment that you may acquire in the future.

5 Tool racks
Store most of your tools on space-saving wall racks, using dowel pegs or metal hooks. Mark the profile of the tool on the wall to help identify its location and signal when it is missing.

6 First-aid kit
Place a well-stocked first-aid kit in an accessible and conspicuous position.

7 Small items
Store small cans and packets on narrow shelves. Keep loose nails and screws in glass jars for easy identification.

8 Workbench
A woodworking bench must be rigid. Make your own wall-mounted bench with sturdy softwood framing, using three layers of man-made board glued together for the worktop. A woodworking vise can be mounted on to the worktop as required. Alternatively, buy a ready-made bench complete with side and end vises (see page 10).

If you plan to use the workshop for car maintenance, too, and lack room for a separate workbench, use plastic-laminated board to make a removable worktop that fits over your woodworking bench. Screw a softwood rail to the front edge and an upstanding rail at the back.

9 Electrical sockets
Have wall-mounted electrical sockets for power tools installed above the worktop.

10 Bench storage
Utilize the space under your workbench for suspended drawers or for cupboards or open shelves, so you can store tools and accessories that are either too heavy or too small to be hung on the wall.

11 Trash can
Stand a mobile waste-collection can next to the workbench. For convenience, line the can with a disposable plastic bag.

12 Scrap box
Keep short lengths of useful material on end in a box or bin. Put on castors to make it easy to move.

13 Assembly area
Leave an area for cutting larger pieces of material, assembling work and applying finishes—supporting the work on a folding bench or trestles.

14 Lighting
Use fluorescent light fixtures to provide even illumination, particularly over the worktop. Choose "daylight" tubes to make color matching of woods easier, and try to make use of natural light from windows. Paint interior surfaces white to reflect more light.

15 Security
Install secure locks on windows and doors, to deter burglars and inquisitive children.

HEALTH AND SAFETY IN THE WORKSHOP

Provided you adopt a sensible attitude toward handling sharp tools, there is no reason why you should have a serious accident in a workshop. Even so, it is advisable to protect yourself from harmful dust, fumes, and, when using power tools, from flying particles and noise.

Safety glasses
Made from tough impact-resistant polycarbonate plastic, safety glasses are designed with sidescreens to protect your eyes from dust and wood particles.

Goggles
The rigid lenses of safety goggles are surrounded with a soft plastic frame that fits and seals against the contours of your face. The sides are ventilated to prevent condensation. Safety goggles can usually be worn over prescription glasses.

Face mask
A face mask stops you from inhaling fine dust. Paper and gauze masks are available, and some have replaceable filters.

Respirator
A professional dual-cartridge respirator provides full protection against the harmful effects of toxic dust and fumes. Interchangeable color-coded cartridges are designed to filter specific materials.

Hearing protectors
Earplugs and padded ear muffs or ear defenders, as they are often called, protect your hearing from overexposure to noise. Always wear protectors when using noisy power tools that could cause long-term damage.

WORKBENCHES

There are numerous commercially made woodworking benches, available in various lengths and widths, but having a standard height of 32 inches; most manufacturers also supply made-to-order benches of any height. The cabinetmaker's bench has the most useful features, including two vises and some form of tool storage.

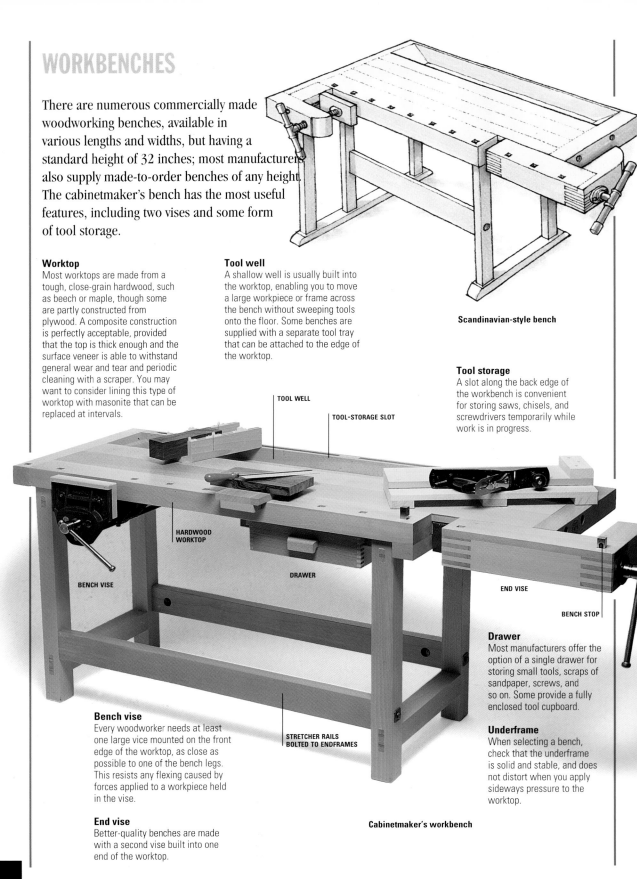

Scandinavian-style bench

Worktop
Most worktops are made from a tough, close-grain hardwood, such as beech or maple, though some are partly constructed from plywood. A composite construction is perfectly acceptable, provided that the top is thick enough and the surface veneer is able to withstand general wear and tear and periodic cleaning with a scraper. You may want to consider lining this type of worktop with masonite that can be replaced at intervals.

Tool well
A shallow well is usually built into the worktop, enabling you to move a large workpiece or frame across the bench without sweeping tools onto the floor. Some benches are supplied with a separate tool tray that can be attached to the edge of the worktop.

Tool storage
A slot along the back edge of the workbench is convenient for storing saws, chisels, and screwdrivers temporarily while work is in progress.

TOOL WELL

TOOL-STORAGE SLOT

HARDWOOD WORKTOP

DRAWER

BENCH VISE

END VISE

BENCH STOP

STRETCHER RAILS BOLTED TO ENDFRAMES

Bench vise
Every woodworker needs at least one large vice mounted on the front edge of the worktop, as close as possible to one of the bench legs. This resists any flexing caused by forces applied to a workpiece held in the vise.

End vise
Better-quality benches are made with a second vise built into one end of the worktop.

Drawer
Most manufacturers offer the option of a single drawer for storing small tools, scraps of sandpaper, screws, and so on. Some provide a fully enclosed tool cupboard.

Underframe
When selecting a bench, check that the underframe is solid and stable, and does not distort when you apply sideways pressure to the worktop.

Cabinetmaker's workbench

Cabinetmaker's benches

Most benches are constructed entirely from hardwood, although less expensive softwoods are sometimes used for the underframe. Underframes are usually constructed from two mortise-and-tenoned endframes joined together with stretcher rails that are securely bolted to the legs. This is a useful feature that allows you to transport the bench more easily. A good-quality bench will have a worktop that is at least 2in (50mm) thick, invariably rectangular, with a vise at the side and at one end.

Folding bench

If you have no workshop or space is limited, you can buy a bench that folds flat for storage. It also doubles as a handy sawhorse in the workshop and as a portable bench for jobs around the house.

The worktop comprises two wide boards that form the vise jaws, one of which can be adjusted to grip tapered or parallel-sided workpieces by turning a crank at each end. On some models, the same jaw can be set vertically to provide downward clamping pressure. Holes drilled in both halves of the worktop accommodate plastic clamping pegs that act as bench stops for gripping awkward-shaped workpieces.

The metal underframe unfolds to standard bench height, but the splayed legs can also be folded under to provide a lower platform for sawing larger workpieces.

WOODWORKING VISES

European-style vises are made with thick wooden jaws to grip the work. Another type of vise has cast-iron jaws lined with wood to protect workpieces from bruising. Both designs are operated by turning a sliding bar on the front jaw. Some metal vises are also equipped with a quick-release lever that disengages part of the screw mechanism, permitting the jaw to be opened and closed rapidly by a straight pull or push.

An end vise provides a clamping force along the bench to hold a workpiece between metal stops dropped into holes cut into the vise and at regular intervals along one or both edges of the worktop.

Continental-style vise

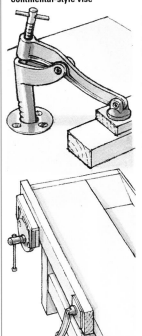

Holdfast

A holdfast is a removable bench-mounted clamp, used to hold a workpiece on the bench top. It has a long shaft that fits into a hole drilled into the top and lined with a metal collar; turning a screw presses a pivoted arm down onto the work.

Clamping a long board

A second collar set into the leg enables you to use a holdfast to support the end of a long board held in the bench vise.

WORKSHOP STORAGE

In the past, woodworkers usually kept their tools in sturdy chests, but it is more convenient to use space-saving tool racks and open shelving. Since there is no need for refined or sophisticated fixtures, workshop storage is relatively easy to make—and you can save yourself a considerable amount of money.

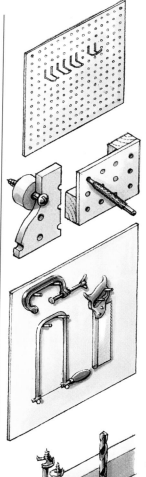

Floor-standing shelving

A floor-standing shelf unit is ideal for heavy materials and equipment. Make the uprights from 2 x 2in (50 x 50mm) planed softwood, joined by 1 x 2in (50 x 25mm) softwood rails bolted across the front and back. Make the shelves from ¾in (18mm) man-made board, not more than 2ft 6in (750mm) wide and 1ft (300mm) deep. Screw stiff metal strips diagonally across the back to brace the frame.

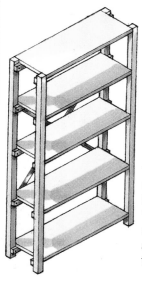

Wall-mounted shelving

Use shallow wall-mounted shelving to store small items. Cut the side panels and shelves from ¾in (18mm) man-made board. Make the unit no more than 3ft (1m) high and 6in (150mm) deep. Cut through housing joints (see page 80) in the side panels for shelves 2ft (600mm) long. In the back corners of the side panels, cut rabbets for top and bottom steadying rails.

Glue and screw the parts together, then screw through the top and bottom rails into the wall.

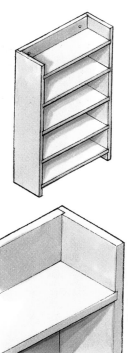

Wire-hook tool rack

To construct a tool rack, use peg board and metal hooks made from wire coat hangers. For lightweight tools, mount a panel ¼in (6mm) thick on the wall, with spacer blocks behind each screw. For heavier tools, pin the panel to a softwood frame.

Pegged tool rack

Cut one or more panels, about 3ft (1m) square, from ½in (12mm) man-made board. Arrange the tools and mark the positions for supporting pegs made from 2 x ½in (50 x 12mm) dowel. Drill locating holes for the pegs at an angle of about 5 degrees, then glue the pegs in place. Screw the panels to the wall.

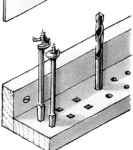

Storing drill bits

Make selecting drill bits easier by storing your collection of bits on end in holes drilled in a block of wood. Stand the block on a shelf, or pin and glue a strip of wood to the back edge of the block s so it can be screwed to a wall.

Containers for small items

To store bits and pieces neatly on shelves, recycle plastic food containers. Mark the tubs with a pen, or use adhesive labels.

Screw-top glass jars make useful containers for loose items like nails, screws, nuts, and bolts. Keep the jars on a slim shelf, or screw their lids the underside of a shelf.

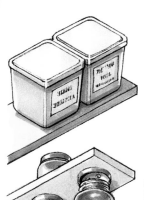

TOOLS
AND BASIC
TECHNIQUES

RULES AND TAPE MEASURES

Since even the best measuring tools are relatively inexpensive, most woodworkers acquire a variety of rules and tape measures to meet different needs. However, it is advisable to use the same rule or tape measure when marking a project, just in case there is any variation between one tool and another. It generally makes sense to buy rules and tape

measures that are made with both standard and metric graduations—but take care not to confuse one system with the other once you have begun to mark out a workpiece. To make sure several identical components are exactly the same size, measure one of them accurately, then use that piece of wood as a template to mark the others.

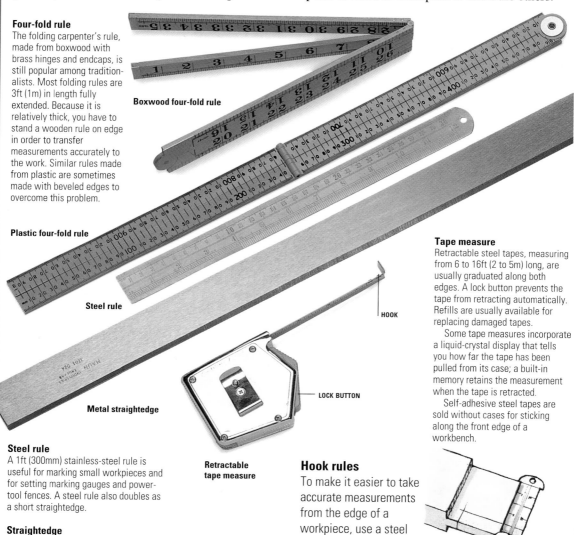

Four-fold rule
The folding carpenter's rule, made from boxwood with brass hinges and endcaps, is still popular among tradition-alists. Most folding rules are 3ft (1m) in length fully extended. Because it is relatively thick, you have to stand a wooden rule on edge in order to transfer measurements accurately to the work. Similar rules made from plastic are sometimes made with beveled edges to overcome this problem.

Boxwood four-fold rule

Plastic four-fold rule

Steel rule

Metal straightedge

HOOK

LOCK BUTTON

Retractable tape measure

Tape measure
Retractable steel tapes, measuring from 6 to 16ft (2 to 5m) long, are usually graduated along both edges. A lock button prevents the tape from retracting automatically. Refills are usually available for replacing damaged tapes.
   Some tape measures incorporate a liquid-crystal display that tells you how far the tape has been pulled from its case; a built-in memory retains the measurement when the tape is retracted.
   Self-adhesive steel tapes are sold without cases for sticking along the front edge of a workbench.

Steel rule
A 1ft (300mm) stainless-steel rule is useful for marking small workpieces and for setting marking gauges and power-tool fences. A steel rule also doubles as a short straightedge.

Straightedge
Every workshop needs at least one sturdy metal straightedge, measuring between 1ft 8in (500mm) and 6ft 6in (2m) long. A beveled straightedge is ideal for making accurate cuts with a marking knife and for checking that a planed surface is perfectly flat. Some straightedges are etched with standard metric and/or graduations.

Hook rules
To make it easier to take accurate measurements from the edge of a workpiece, use a steel rule with an integral hook at one end.

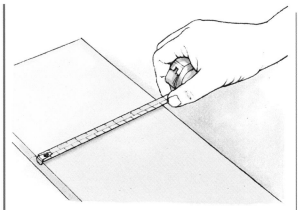

Measuring from edge to edge
When taking external measurements with a tape measure, hook the tip over one edge of the workpiece and read the dimension against the opposite edge.

Taking internal measurements
When measuring between two components, the hook riveted to a retractable tape measure slides backward to align with the tip of the tape. Read the dimension where the tape enters its case, then add the length of the case to arrive at the true measurement.

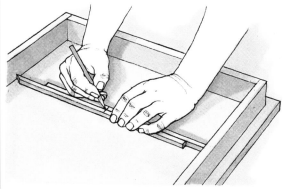

Using pinch rods
Another way to gauge the distance between components is to bridge the gap with two strips of wood held side by side. Draw a mark across both strips to register their relative positions—then, without releasing your grip, transfer them to the work.

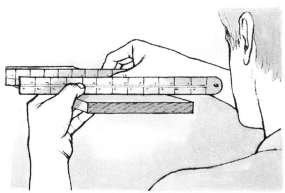

Checking for winding
If you suspect a board is twisted or "winding", hold a steel rule across each end; if the rules appear to be parallel, the board is flat.

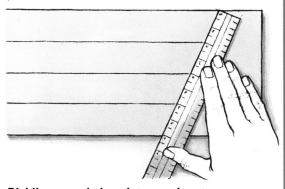

Dividing a workpiece into equal parts
You can divide a workpiece into equal parts using any rule or tape measure. To divide a board into quarters, for example, align the tip of the rule with one edge and the fourth division with the opposite edge, then mark off the divisions between.

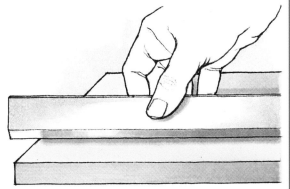

Checking that a surface is flat
To check that a panel is flat, place a straightedge on the surface. A bump will cause the tool to rock; chinks of light showing beneath the straightedge indicate hollows. Turn the straightedge to various angles to gauge whether the entire surface is flat.

SQUARES AND BEVELS

Squares and sliding bevels are used by woodworkers to mark workpieces and to check the accuracy of individual components and assemblies.

Trysquare
The finest trysquares, used to mark and check right angles, have a blued-steel metal blade riveted at 90 degrees to a rosewood stock edged with brass. A square with a 1ft (300mm) blade is best for general woodwork, but you might find a smaller, all-metal engineer's square useful for fine work and for setting up power tools.

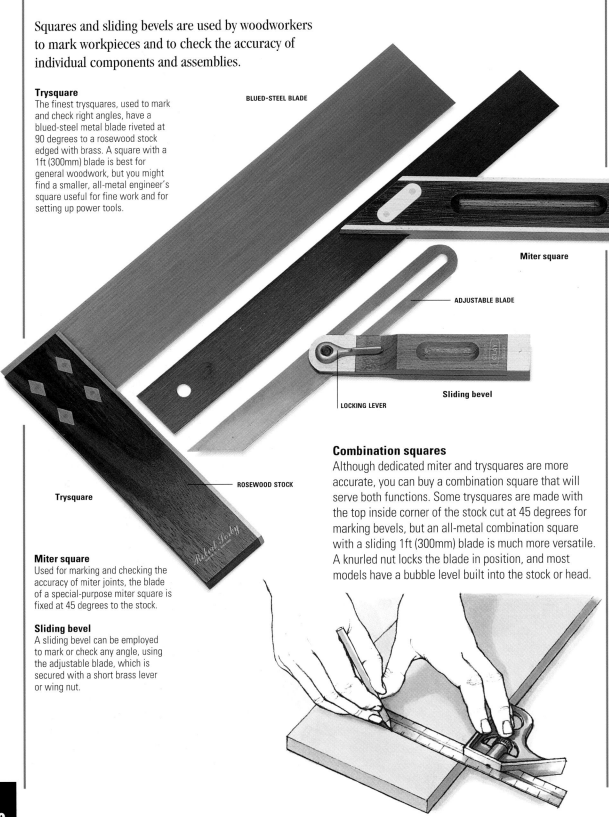

BLUED-STEEL BLADE

Miter square

ADJUSTABLE BLADE

Sliding bevel

LOCKING LEVER

ROSEWOOD STOCK

Trysquare

Miter square
Used for marking and checking the accuracy of miter joints, the blade of a special-purpose miter square is fixed at 45 degrees to the stock.

Sliding bevel
A sliding bevel can be employed to mark or check any angle, using the adjustable blade, which is secured with a short brass lever or wing nut.

Combination squares
Although dedicated miter and trysquares are more accurate, you can buy a combination square that will serve both functions. Some trysquares are made with the top inside corner of the stock cut at 45 degrees for marking bevels, but an all-metal combination square with a sliding 1ft (300mm) blade is much more versatile. A knurled nut locks the blade in position, and most models have a bubble level built into the stock or head.

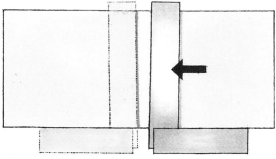

Checking the accuracy of a trysquare

From time to time, it pays to check the accuracy of your trysquare—this is especially important when using a combination square that does not have a fixed blade. Draw a line at right angles to the edge of a workpiece, turn the square over, and slide the blade up to the marked line. The blade and the pencil mark will align precisely if the square is accurate.

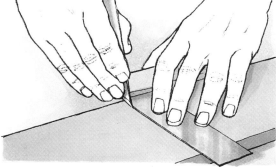

Marking with a trysquare

Mark square shoulders with a trysquare. Use a pencil for the first stages of marking joints, but always use a marking knife, beveled on one side of the blade, to sever the wood fibers along lines that are to be sawn or chiseled.

Place the tip of the knife on the pencil line, and slide the square up to the flat side of the blade. Holding the square firmly against the face edge, push the knife along the marked line.

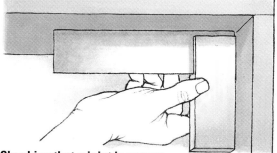

Checking that a joint is square

When assembling corner joints, use a trysquare to check that the two components meet at a right angle.

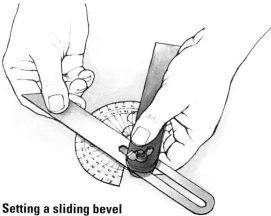

Setting a sliding bevel

Slacken the locking lever just enough for the blade to move; set the required angle against a protractor, then retighten the lever.

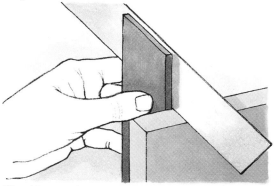

Checking a miter or bevel

Place a miter square or sliding bevel over the beveled face of a workpiece. Keeping the blade in contact with the wood, slide the tool along the beveled face to check the angle's accuracy across the width of the workpiece.

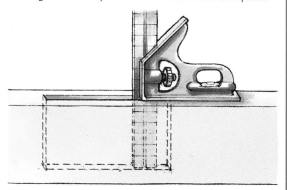

Using a square as a depth gauge

Measure the depth of a mortise with a combination square. Slacken the knurled nut, then place the tip of the blade against the bottom of the mortise and slide the head up against the edge of the work. Remove the tool and read the depth of the mortise against the inside edge of the head.

MARKING GAUGES

Gauges are designed to score fine lines parallel with the edges of a workpiece, usually for marking joints or scribing rabbets.

Marking gauge
A marking gauge comprises an adjustable fence or stock that slides along a hardwood beam that has a sharp steel pin driven through one end. A thumbscrew clamps the stock at any point along the beam. Better-quality gauges have brass strips set flush with the running face of the stock to prevent wear.

Mortise gauge
A mortise gauge is made with two pins, one fixed and the other adjustable, so that you can score both sides of a mortise simultaneously. On the best gauges the movable pin is adjustable to very fine tolerances, using a thumbscrew located at the end of the beam. Most mortise gauges have a second fixed pin on the back of the beam so the tool can double as a standard marking gauge.

Cutting gauge
A cutting gauge is equipped with a miniature blade instead of a pointed pin, enabling you to mark a line across the grain without tearing the wood fibers. The blade, which is held in place with a brass wedge, can be removed for sharpening. A standard scribing blade, used for marking various corner joints, has a rounded cutting tip. Substitute a pointed knife-edge blade for trimming strips of veneer.

Curved-edge gauge
It is practically impossible to score a line parallel to a curved edge with an ordinary marking gauge. A curved-edge gauge has a brass fence that rests on two points, preventing the stock from rocking as it follows the edge of the work. The same tool can also be used on straight edges.

Panel gauge
A standard marking gauge has a 8in (200mm) beam, but there are special gauges with beams up to 2ft 8in (800mm) long for scribing lines on man-made boards. These panel gauges have relatively wide stocks, held in place with a captive wedge or a wooden clamping screw.

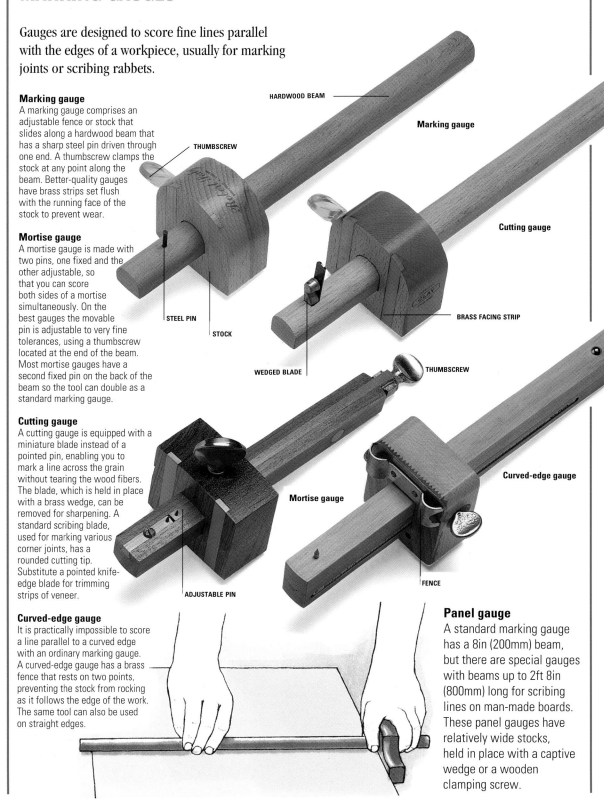

HARDWOOD BEAM

Marking gauge

THUMBSCREW

Cutting gauge

STEEL PIN

STOCK

WEDGED BLADE

BRASS FACING STRIP

THUMBSCREW

Mortise gauge

Curved-edge gauge

ADJUSTABLE PIN

FENCE

1 Setting a marking gauge

Some marking gauges have graduated beams that make it easy to adjust the stock, but it is usually necessary to align the pin with a rule, then slide the stock with your thumb until it comes to rest against the end of the rule.

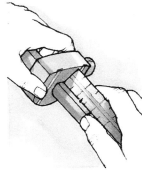

2 Adjusting a marking gauge

Tighten the thumbscrew and check the setting. If necessary, make fine adjustments by tapping the base of the beam against a bench to increase the distance between pin and stock. Reduce this distance by tapping the tip.

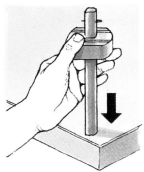

Setting a mortise gauge

Adjust the distance between the pins to match the width of a mortise chisel, then set the stock to suit the thickness of the leg or stile. Use the same pin setting to scribe a matching tenon, adjusting the stock accordingly.

Scribing with a gauge

Place the beam on the workpiece with the pin pointing toward you, then slide the stock up against the side of the work. Rotate the tool until the pin begins to mark the wood; then push the gauge away from you to scribe a clear line.

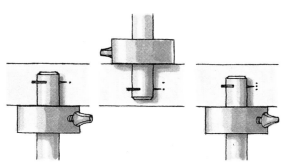

Gauging a center line

To find the exact center of a rail or stile, set a marking gauge as accurately as possible, then check the measurement by making a single pin prick, first from one side of the workpiece, then from the other. If the pin pricks fall short or overshoot the center line, adjust the gauge until they coincide.

IMPROVISING A GAUGE

For carpentry that does not require absolute precision, you can gauge lines with a pencil.

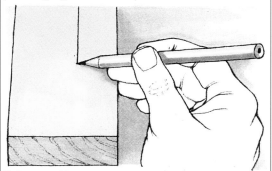

Using your fingertip

Run a fingertip against the edge of the workpiece to keep the pencil point on a parallel path.

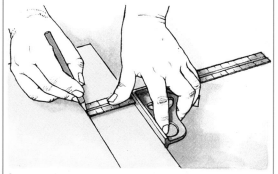

Gauging with a combination square

For slightly wider dimensions, follow the edge of the work with the head of a combination square, using the tip of the blade to guide the pencil point.

SAWS

Saws are designed for converting planks of solid wood and man-made boards into smaller components, ready for planing. The very best saws are skew-backed, having a gentle S-bend to the top of the blade that reduces the weight of the saw and improves its balance. The same blades are usually hollow ground and reduced in thickness above the cutting edge to provide better clearance in the kerf.

Skew-back, hollow-ground handsaw

Rip saw

The largest hand saw, with a 2ft 2in (650mm) blade, is designed specifically for cutting solid lumber in the direction of the grain. A rip saw has large teeth with almost vertical leading edges, and each tooth is filed straight across to produce a chisellike cutting tip. In common with all but the smallest saws, alternate teeth are "set", or bent to the right or left, to cut a kerf that is wider than the thickness of the blade. This prevents the saw from jamming in the wood. Rip saws are made with 5 or 6 PPI (see opposite).

Rip saw

Crosscut saw

A crosscut saw has teeth specially designed for severing solid wood across the grain, and is therefore the ideal saw for cutting planks or lumber posts to length. Each tooth leans backward at an angle or "pitch" of 14 degrees, and is filed with a sharp cutting edge and tip that score the wood fibres on each side of the kerf. Crosscut-saw blades are between 2 to 2ft 2in (600 and 650mm) long, with 7 to 8 PPI.

Crosscut saw

Panel saw

Having relatively small crosscut teeth, at 10 PPI, a panel saw is designed primarily for cutting man-made boards to size, but doubles as a crosscut saw for severing solid wood. Panel-saw blades are between 1ft 8in and 1ft 10in (500 and 550mm) long.

Panel saw

Universal saw

Some manufacturers offer universal handsaws with teeth that are similar in shape to those of a crosscut saw, but which cut well both with and across the grain. Universal saws are made with 6 to 10 PPI.

Fleam-tooth saws

Fleam-tooth crosscutting saws are particularly efficient because they sever the wood on the return stroke as well as the forward. Fleam teeth have a pitch of 22.5 degrees.

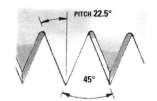

PITCH **22.5°**

45°

Hardened saw teeth

Modern saws are sometimes subjected to a high-frequency hardening process. A hardpoint saw, which is distinguishable by its blue-black toothed edge, stays sharp longer than an untreated saw, but the metal is so hard the teeth have to be sharpened by a specialist.

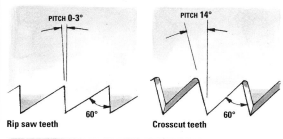

Rip saw teeth PITCH 0-3° 60°

Crosscut teeth PITCH 14° 60°

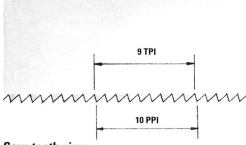

9 TPI

10 PPI

Saw-tooth sizes

Saw-tooth sizes are generally specified by the number of teeth that fit into 1 inch—TPI (teeth per inch)—measuring from the base of one tooth to the base of another. Alternatively, saw teeth may be specified by PPI (points per inch) counting the number of saw-tooth tips in 1 inch of blade. When compared, there is always one more PPI than TPI.

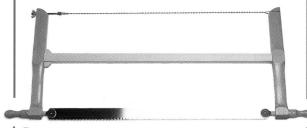

Frame saw

Although it resembles some curve-cutting saws (see page 25), a traditional-style frame saw is designed for ripping or crosscutting solid wood, depending on which blade is used. The narrow blade is held under tension by a twisted-wire tourniquet that runs between the solid-wood end posts or "cheeks". The frame can be swung to one side to provide clearance when ripping boards to width.

SAW HANDLES

Elegant handles are still made from tough short-grain hardwood, although the majority of hand saws now have molded plastic grips that are more economical to manufacture. The choice of material makes no difference to the performance of the saw, but make sure the handle feels comfortable to hold and check that it is set low behind the blade for maximum thrust on the forward stroke.

Open and closed grips

Some small dovetail saws and keyhole saws are made with open pistol-grip handles. However, most saws are made with stronger closed handgrips.

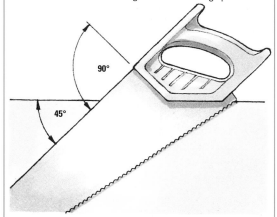

90°

45°

Using a saw as a square

Plastic handles are sometimes molded with shoulders set at 90 and 45 degrees to the straight back of the blade so the saw can be used as a large trysquare or miter square.

Caring for handsaws

Saw teeth dull quickly if saws are thrown carelessly into a tool box or if one saw blade is dragged across another. Slip a plastic guard over the toothed edge of a blade before storing it, or carry your saws in a canvas case that is made with separate pockets to house a selection of saws.

Use mineral spirits to clean resin deposits from a saw blade, and wipe the metal with an oily rag before you put it away.

USING SAWS

Provided the saw is sharp and the teeth have been set properly, it is possible to work for long periods with a saw without tiring.

The best grip
Hold a saw with your index finger extended toward the toe of the blade. This grip provides optimum control over the direction of cut and prevents the handle from twisting in the palm of your hand.

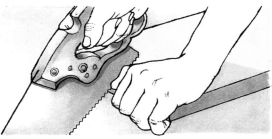

Starting the cut
Place the cutting edge of the saw just to the waste side of the marked line. Guiding the saw with your thumb held against the flat of the blade, make short backward strokes to establish the cut.

Following through
Saw with slow, steady strokes, using the full length of the blade—fast or erratic movements can be tiring, and the saw is more inclined to jam or wander off line.

If the cut does begin to deviate from the intended course, twist the blade slightly to bring it back on line. If you find a saw consistently wanders, make sure that the teeth are set accurately.

Prevent the saw from jamming
If the kerf begins to close on the blade, drive a small wedge into the cut to keep it open. Otherwise, lubricate the saw by rubbing a candle on both sides of the blade.

Finishing the cut
As you approach the end of a cut, lower the saw handle slightly and make slow, deliberate strokes as you sever the last few wood fibers. Support a long offcut with your free hand, or ask someone else to take the weight while you finish sawing.

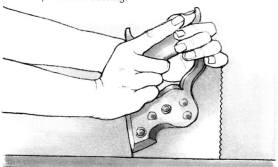

Reverse-action grip
To finish sawing a large panel or ripping a long plank of wood, turn around and saw back toward the kerf you have just made. Alternatively, use a two-handed grip to control the saw, continuing the kerf in the same direction, but with the saw teeth facing away from you.

SUPPORTING THE WORK

You cannot hope to cut a workpiece with accuracy unless you support it properly. You can clamp a piece of wood to a bench top, but you may find it more comfortable to use a pair of trestles or sawhorses about 2ft (600mm) high, which will allow you to hold the work down with one hand and use your knee to stop it from swiveling.

Crosscutting
Bridge a pair of sawhorses with a plank of wood for crosscutting. If the workpiece is thin and whippy, support it from beneath with a thicker piece of wood. Clamp a short plank to the top of a single sawhorse.

Crosscutting with a frame saw
When severing a plank of wood with a frame saw, cant the frame slightly to one side so that you can see the cut line clearly. Pass your free hand through the frame and behind the blade to support an offcut.

Ripping with a frame saw
Clamp the work to a sturdy bench, so you can use two hands to control the saw, and turn the blade at 90 degrees to the frame. Grip one of the end posts with both hands to make sure the narrow blade cannot twist and cause the saw to wander off line.

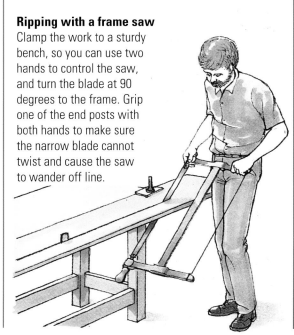

Ripsawing
Support the work in a similar way when ripping a plank lengthwise, moving each sawhorse in turn to provide a clear path for the blade. Prevent a wide man-made panel from flexing by placing two planks under the board, one on each side of the kerf.

BACKSAWS

Backsaws are made with relatively small crosscut teeth for trimming lengths of wood to size and for cutting woodworking joints. The special feature of all backsaws is the heavy steel or brass strip folded over the top of the blade. This strip of metal not only keeps the blade straight enough but provides weight to keep the teeth in contact with the wood without having to force the blade into the work.

Tenon saw
A tenon saw, having 13 to 15 PPI along a 10 to 14in (250 to 350mm) blade, is the largest and most versatile of the backsaw family. While it is possible to sever fairly hefty sections of lumber with a tenon saw, it is also a suitable saw for precise work such as cutting tenons and other large woodworking joints.

Dovetail saw
A dovetail saw is a smaller version of the tenon saw, but the teeth are too fine—16 to 22 PPI—to be set conventionally, relying instead on the bur produced by file-sharpening to provide the extremely narrow kerf required for cutting dovetails and similar joints. Dovetail saws with traditional closed or pistol-grip handles are generally made with 8in (200mm) blades. An alternative-pattern saw, with a longer blade, has a straight handle in line with the folded metal strip.

Offset dovetail saw
A straight dovetail saw with a handle cranked to one side is made for trimming dowels and through tenons flush with the wood surface.

Bead saw
A miniature backsaw with about 26 PPI, the bead saw is ideal for cutting extremely fine joints and for model making.

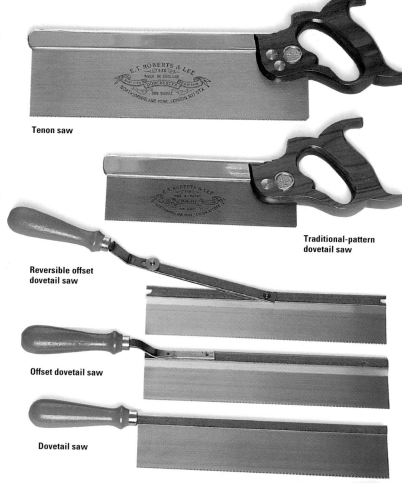

Tenon saw

Traditional-pattern dovetail saw

Reversible offset dovetail saw

Offset dovetail saw

Dovetail saw

Bead saw

Cutting with the grain
Clamp the work in a bench vise when sawing a tenon or dovetail down to the shoulder.

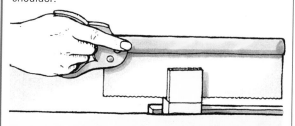

Crosscutting
Holding the work securely against a bench hook (see page 84), make short backward strokes on the waste side of the line until the cut is established; then gradually lower the blade to the horizontal as you extend the kerf.

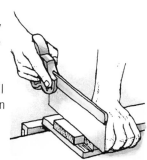

CURVE-CUTTING SAWS

A group of saws with narrow blades is made specifically for cutting curved shapes or holes in solid wood and boards. Various sizes and designs are available; your choice will depend on the material to be cut and the scale of the work.

Bow saw
A medium-weight frame saw suitable for cutting relatively thick pieces of wood, the bow saw is fitted with an 8 to 12in (200 to 300mm) blade, held under tension by a tourniquet that runs between the saw's end posts. The 9 to 17 PPI blades can be turned 360 degrees to swing the frame aside.

Coping saw
The very narrow blade of a 6in (150mm) coping saw is held under tension by the spring of its metal frame. The 15 to 17 PPI blades are too narrow to sharpen and are simply replaced when they become blunt or broken. A coping saw blade can be turned to swing the frame out of the way to facilitate cutting curves in either solid wood or man-made boards.

Fret saw
Similar in construction to a coping saw, the fret saw has a deep frame that holds replaceable blades under tension. A fret saw, with its 32 PPI blades, is for cutting thin pieces of wood and board, or for shaping a sandwich of marquetry veneers. A fret saw cuts on the pull stroke to prevent the blade from buckling.

Compass saw
Most curve-cutting saws are limited by their frames to cutting holes relatively close to the edges of a workpiece. A compass saw has a narrow, tapered blade that is stiff enough to hold its shape without being held under tension and, as a result, can be used to cut a hole in a board of any thickness as far from the edges as required. The 8 to 10 PPI blades are either bolted into a pistol-grip handle or set into a straight handle that is convenient for turning the saw to cut in any direction.

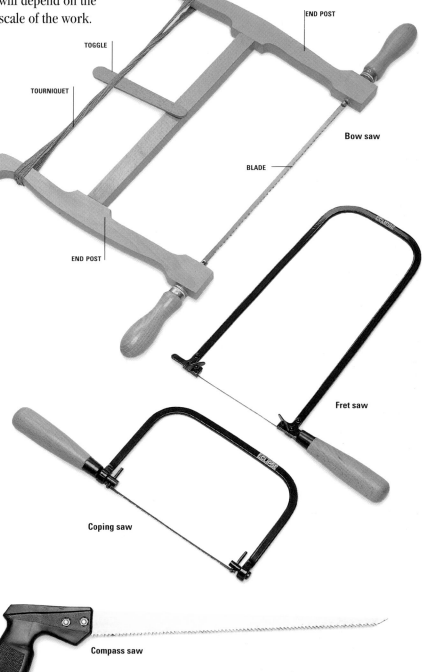

END POST

TOGGLE

TOURNIQUET

BLADE

Bow saw

END POST

Fret saw

Coping saw

Compass saw

PISTOL-GRIP HANDLE

USING CURVE-CUTTING SAWS

Most curve-cutting saws require special techniques to counter the tendency for the weight of their frames to turn the blade off line.

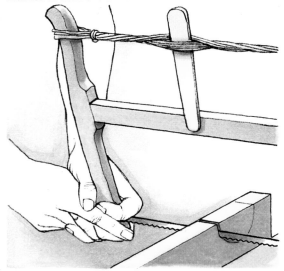

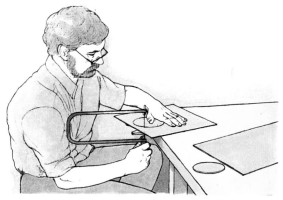

Using a fret saw
Thin workpieces tend to vibrate unless they are supported from below by a strip of plywood screwed to the bench top, overhanging the front edge. Cut a V-shape notch in the plywood to provide clearance for the fret-saw blade. So that you can cut downward on the pull stroke, sit on a low stool with your chest at about bench height.

Cutting with a bow saw
A bow saw requires a two-handed grip to control the direction of cut and compensate for the twisting force of the frame. Grip the straight handle with one hand, extending your index finger in line with the blade. Place your free hand alongside the other, wrapping the index finger and middle finger around the saw's end post, one on each side of the blade.

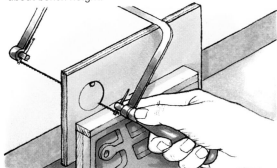

Making closed cuts
When cutting a hole with any frame saw, mark the work and bore a small access hole for the blade, just inside the waste. Pass the saw blade through the hole and connect it to the frame.

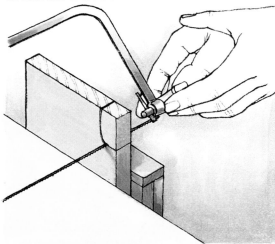

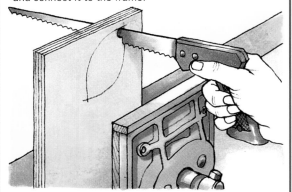

Controlling a coping saw
To prevent the blade from wandering off line, place the first joint of your extended index finger on the coping saw's frame. For greater comfort, close your other hand around the first to form a double-handed grip.

Sawing holes with a compass saw
When cutting holes with a compass saw, drill a starter hole for the tip of the blade. Saw steadily to avoid buckling the blade on the forward stroke.

REPLACING BLADES

Curve-cutting saws are designed for quick and easy replacement of blunt, broken, or bent blades.

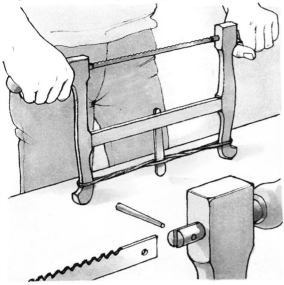

Changing a bow-saw blade
Unwind the toggle to slacken the tourniquet, then locate each end of the blade in the slotted metal rods that extend from the handles. Pass the tapered retaining pins through the rods and blade at both ends. Tighten the tourniquet again and rotate both handles to straighten the blade.

Putting in a compass-saw blade
To fit a compass-saw blade, slacken the screw bolts and slide the slotted end of the replacement blade into the handle. Tighten both bolts.

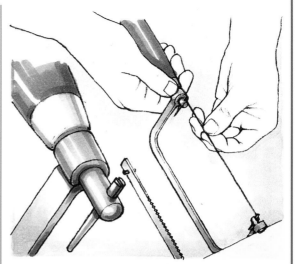

Replacing a damaged coping-saw blade
Each end of a coping-saw blade fits into a slotted retaining pin. To replace a damaged blade, reduce the distance between the retaining pins by turning the saw's handle counterclockwise; hold the pin attached to the handle between finger and thumb to prevent it from spinning.

Attach the blade to the toe of the saw, with the teeth facing away from the handle. Flex the frame against the edge of a bench until you can locate the other end of the blade. Holding its retaining pin as before, tighten the handle to tension the blade; then align both pins by eye.

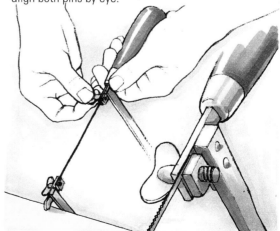

Putting in a fret-saw blade
Fret-saw blades are put in in a similar way, but instead of retaining pins, a thumbscrew clamps the flat section at each end of a blade. With the teeth facing the handle, clamp the toe end of the blade, then flex the frame against a bench, tightening the other thumbscrew onto the blade. Releasing pressure on the frame is enough to put the blade under tension.

HAMMERS AND MALLETS

Most workshops boast a range of hammers, even though they are rarely used in joint-making, except when reinforcing with pins or nails.

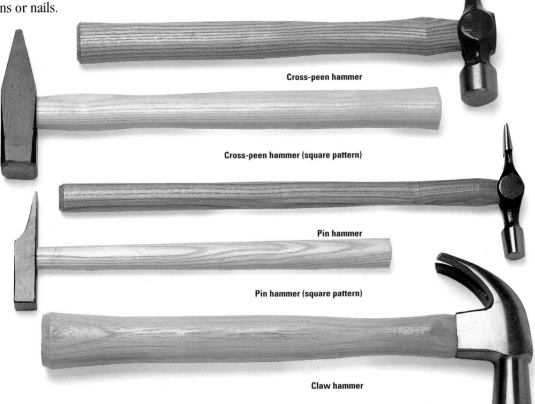

Cross-peen hammer

Cross-peen hammer (square pattern)

Pin hammer

Pin hammer (square pattern)

Claw hammer

Cross-peen hammer
One medium-weight cross-peen hammer will suffice for most needs. It is heavy enough to tap joints together and dismantle them again, yet well balanced enough so that you can perform precise operations, such as starting a nail or panel pin with the wedge-shape peen on the back of the hammer head.

Pin hammer
For delicate work, such as nailing small picture-frame miters, use a lightweight cross-peen pin hammer.

Claw hammer
You will find a claw hammer convenient for making jigs and mock-ups from softwood. Not only can you drive in large nails with ease, but you can also extract them with the split peen, using the strong shaft as a lever. Though slightly more expensive, all-metal claw hammers are even stronger than those with wooden shafts.

Nail punch
A nail punch is a tapered metal tool that is used with a hammer to drive nail heads below a wood surface.

Carpenter's mallet
Although you can drive plastic-handle chisels and gouges with a metal hammer, you will need to use a mallet for those with wooden handles, to prevent them from splitting. This tool is specially designed for the job; its wide head is tapered so it will strike a chisel squarely each time, and will wedge itself even more securely on the tapered shaft with each blow.

CHISELS AND GOUGES

Woodworking of any kind is impossible without at least a small range of well-made chisels and gouges. In joint-making, they are especially useful for removing waste wood and for paring components to make a snug fit.

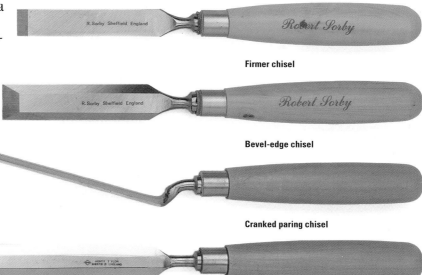

Firmer chisel

Bevel-edge chisel

Cranked paring chisel

Paring chisel

Sash-mortise chisel

Firmer chisel
The standard woodworking chisel has a strong rectangular-section blade which you can confidently drive with a mallet through pine or hardwoods, without fear of it breaking. Firmer chisels range from ⅛ to 1½in (3 to 38mm) wide.

Bevel-edge chisel
The slim-bladed bevel-edge chisel is designed for more delicate work, using hand pressure only. It is used primarily for shaping and trimming joints, and the bevels ground along both sides of the blade make the chisel suitable for working dovetail undercuts. Bevel-edge chisels are made in the same widths as firmers.

Paring chisel
A paring chisel is a bevel-edge chisel with an extra-long blade for leveling housings. A cranked version makes it possible to pare waste from very wide joints.

Sash-mortise chisel
This is a specialized chisel for cutting deep mortises. It is made with a tapered blade that does not jam in the work, and which is thick enough to be used as a lever when chopping waste out of a joint. The deep blade sides help keep it square to the mortise. Mortise chisels are made up to ½in (12mm) wide.

Firmer gouges
A gouge is a chisel with a blade curved in cross section. When the cutting-edge bevel is ground on the inside of the blade, it is known as an in-cannel gouge; the tip of an out-cannel blade is ground on the outside. Gouges are used to scoop waste wood out of hollows and to trim curved shoulders. They average from ¼ to 1in (6 to 25mm) wide.

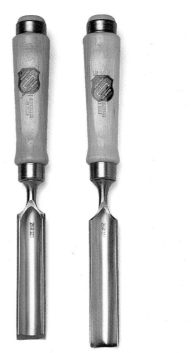

In-cannel gouge   **Out-cannel gouge**

PLANES

Bench planes are general-purpose tools used to smooth the surfaces of lumber and to plane it square and true. Wooden planes are still available, but nearly all planes are now made from metal. In addition, you will need a few specialized planes for shaping and trimming joints.

Jack plane

Metal smoothing plane

Wooden smoothing plane

Rabbet plane
This is no longer an essential tool, now that power routers are widespread, but rabbeting is surprisingly fast by hand. The plane has an adjustable fence and depth stop; with the blade mounted near the toe, you can cut stopped rabbets. The pointed spur mounted on the side of the plane scores the wood ahead of the blade when rabbeting across the grain.

Jack plane
The 1ft 2in (350mm) jack plane is long enough to plane most edges accurately. An even longer version, the try plane, is perfect for preparing edge-to-edge butt joints, but is expensive, so most woodworkers manage with the jack plane.

Smoothing plane
The smoothing plane is the smallest bench plane available, at 9in (225mm) long, and is ideal for final shaping and finishing of workpieces. Some woodworkers prefer the feel of a wooden smoothing plane, with its distinctive ergonomic grip and lignum-vitae sole.

Shoulder plane (top)
A dedicated joint-cutting tool, the all-metal shoulder plane is designed specifically for shaving square shoulders on larger joints. Its blade is set at a low angle to enable it to slice through end grain.

Bullnose plane (above)
A miniature version of the shoulder plane, the bullnose plane is useful for trimming small joints.

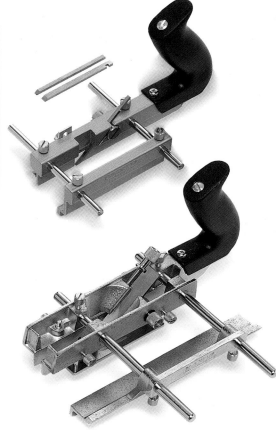

Block plane
A block plane is small enough to be used single-handedly, yet strong enough to take generous shavings for fast shaping and trimming. It is a good general-purpose plane, much used for cutting end grain.

Plow plane (top)
An inexpensive plane, used for cutting narrow grooves parallel with an edge, this comes with a range of interchangeable cutters, from ⅛ to ½in (3 to 12mm) wide. Plow planes are equipped with a strong side fence and a depth stop.

Combination plane (above)
The sophisticated combination plane cuts even wider grooves than a plow plane and can be used to shape a matching tongue along the edge of another component. The tool can also be modified to plane a raised bead along a tongued edge.

Router plane (left)
Once the preferred tool for leveling housings and hinge recesses, the hand router plane has largely been superseded by the power router. Nevertheless, because of its relative cheapness and simplicity, it is still a worthy tool, capable of very accurate work. Special adjustable cutters are made for leveling square and dovetail housings.

DISMANTLING AND ADJUSTING BENCH PLANES

All metal bench planes are made with similar components and are dismantled in the same way. In some planes, the blade is held in place with a wedge, although most modern planes made from wood have capped blades and depth-adjustment screws.

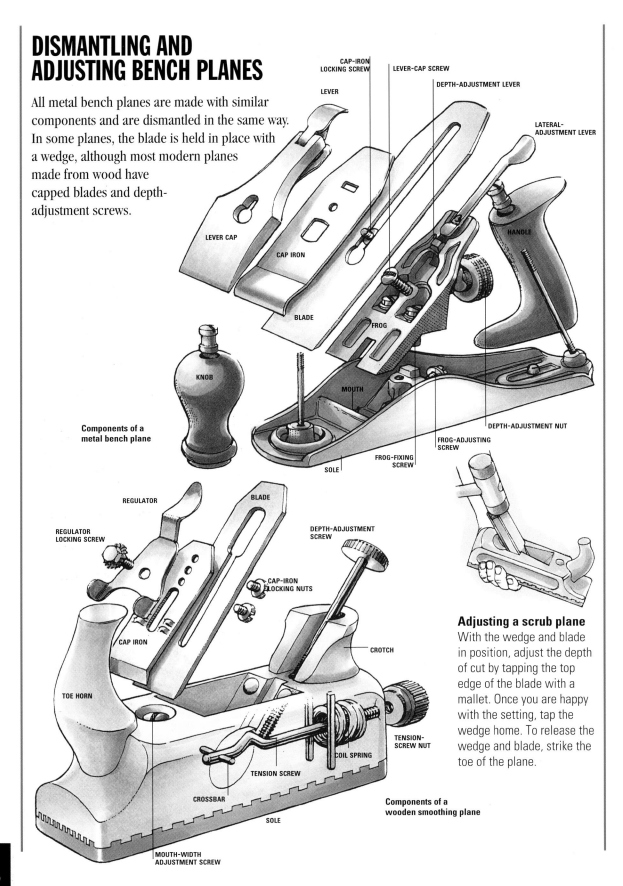

CAP-IRON LOCKING SCREW

LEVER

LEVER-CAP SCREW

DEPTH-ADJUSTMENT LEVER

LATERAL-ADJUSTMENT LEVER

LEVER CAP

CAP IRON

HANDLE

BLADE

FROG

KNOB

MOUTH

DEPTH-ADJUSTMENT NUT

Components of a metal bench plane

FROG-ADJUSTING SCREW

FROG-FIXING SCREW

SOLE

REGULATOR

BLADE

REGULATOR LOCKING SCREW

DEPTH-ADJUSTMENT SCREW

CAP-IRON LOCKING NUTS

CAP IRON

CROTCH

TOE HORN

TENSION-SCREW NUT

COIL SPRING

TENSION SCREW

CROSSBAR

SOLE

Components of a wooden smoothing plane

MOUTH-WIDTH ADJUSTMENT SCREW

Adjusting a scrub plane

With the wedge and blade in position, adjust the depth of cut by tapping the top edge of the blade with a mallet. Once you are happy with the setting, tap the wedge home. To release the wedge and blade, strike the toe of the plane.

Removing the blade and cap iron

To remove the blade for sharpening or to make other adjustments to a metal bench plane, first take off the lever cap by lifting its lever and sliding the cap backward to release it from its locking screw. Lift the blade and cap iron out of the plane, revealing the wedge-shaped casting known as the frog, which incorporates the blade-depth and lateral-adjustment controls.

To separate the cap iron and blade, use a large screwdriver to loosen the locking screw, then slide the cap iron toward the cutting edge until the screw head can pass through the hole in the blade.

Adjusting the frog

The cutting edge of the blade protrudes through an opening in the sole called the mouth. By adjusting the frog, you can modify the size of this opening to suit the thickness of the wood shavings you want to remove. When coarse planing, for example, open the mouth to provide adequate clearance for thick shavings. Close the mouth when taking fine shavings to encourage them to break and curl against the cap iron.

To slide the frog forward or backward, release its two fixing screws, then turn the frog-adjusting screw with a screwdriver.

Removing the blade from a wooden plane

Back-off the depth-adjustment screw by about ½in (10mm), and loosen the tension-screw nut at the heel of the plane. Turn the tension screw's crossbar through 90 degrees to release the blade assembly, which includes the cap iron and regulator. To dismantle the assembly for sharpening, remove the two screws at the back of the blade.

Assembling and adjusting a wooden plane

Having sharpened the blade (see pages 38—9), replace the cap iron and lower the assembly into the plane. Pass the crossbar through the slot in the assembly, turning the bar to locate it in its seat in the cap iron, then slightly tighten the tension-screw nut.

Adjust the depth screw until the blade protrudes through the mouth of the blade and use the regulator to make sure the cutting edge is parallel with the sole. Back off the depth adjuster to the required setting and finally tighten the tension-screw nut.

To open or close the mouth on a wooden plane, adjust the screw behind the toe horn.

ASSEMBLING A METAL-PLANE BLADE AND CAP IRON

Having sharpened the blade, replace the cap iron and insert the assembly in the plane before making the necessary adjustments.

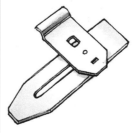

1 Placing the cap iron on the blade

Holding the blade bevel-downward, lay the cap iron across it and locate the head of the captive locking screw in the hole in the blade.

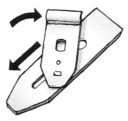

2 Aligning cap iron and blade

Sliding the screw along the slot in the blade, swivel the cap iron until it aligns with the blade. Don't drag the cap iron across the cutting edge.

3 Sliding iron forward

Slide the cap iron to within ¹⁄₁₆in (1mm) or less of the cutting edge and tighten the locking screw.

4 Inserting the blade assembly

Lower the blade assembly into the plane, fitting it over the projecting lever-cap screw and onto the stub of the depth-adjustment lever. Replace the lever cap.

5 Adjusting the blade

Turn the depth-adjustment nut until the blade protrudes from the mouth. Looking along the sole from the toe, move the lateral-adjustment lever until the cutting edge appears to be parallel with the sole. Set the depth of cut.

SERVICING BENCH PLANES

You may experience minor difficulties from time to time, but, provided you take reasonable care of your bench planes, they should require very little servicing except for sharpening. Keep planes clean and well lubricated, and occasionally wipe exposed metal surfaces with an oily rag. Store bench planes on their sides, with their blades withdrawn.

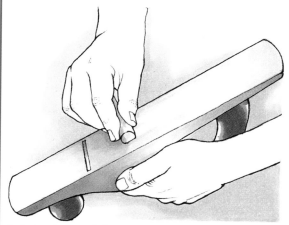

Lubricating a sticky sole
Wooden planes tend to become slick with regular use and rarely need any form of lubrication. However, if you feel that a metal plane is not gliding across the work as it should, lightly rub a stub of white candle across the sole.

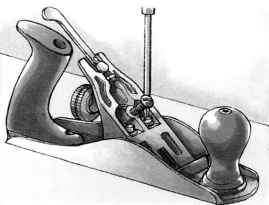

Correcting blade chatter
If your plane vibrates, or "chatters", instead of taking a shaving smoothly, check that the blade is held securely. Tighten the lever-cap screw or, if you are using a wooden plane, the tension-screw nut.

If the fault persists, check that there are no foreign bodies trapped behind the blade and, on a metal bench plane, tighten the frog's fixing screws.

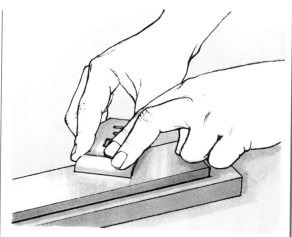

Preventing shavings jamming under the cap iron
Shavings get caught between the leading edge of the cap iron and the blade when these are not fitting snugly against one another. Check that the back of the blade is perfectly flat and that there are no deposits of resin that would prevent the cap iron from bedding down. If the blade is bent, lay it on a flat board and strike it firmly with a hammer.

Re-dress the leading edge of the cap iron on an oilstone, taking care to hone the edge flat and at the original angle.

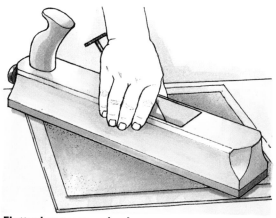

Flattening a warped sole
If your plane seems incapable of taking a thin shaving, lay a metal straightedge across the sole to check that it is not warped. You can correct a warped metal plane by rubbing its sole on a sheet of emery paper or cloth held down on a piece of thick glass with double-sided tape. However, before undertaking such a long, laborious process, it is worth checking whether you can have the plane reground by a professional.

Flattening a wooden sole on abrasive paper is much easier. Remove the blade and, holding the plane near its center, rub the sole back and forth across the paper, checking it regularly with a straightedge.

USING BENCH PLANES

When setting up a workpiece for planing, inspect the wood to ascertain the general direction of the grain. Planing with the grain is always preferable, since planing in the opposite direction tends to tear the wood fibers. If you are planing wood with irregular grain, adjust the bench plane to take very fine shavings.

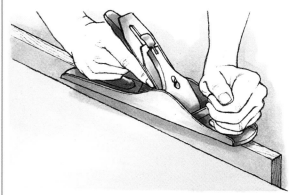

Handling a metal plane

Grasp the handle of a metal bench plane with your index finger extended toward the toe of the tool — this guarantees control over the direction of the plane. Place your free hand on the round knob to hold the toe down on the work.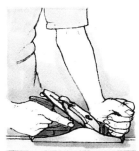

Handling a wooden smoothing plane

Nestle your hand into the shaped crotch just above the heel of the plane, grasping the body with your fingers and thumb. Use the ergonomic horn to provide downward pressure.

The planing action

Stand beside the bench with your feet apart, your rear foot pointing toward the bench, and the other parallel with it. With your feet firmly planted, move your upper body to propel the plane forward. Keep the weight on the toe of the plane as you begin the stroke, transferring pressure to the heel to prevent the plane from rounding off the work at the far end.

Using a slicing action

It is sometimes easier to smooth irregular grain if you create a slicing action by turning the plane at a slight angle to the direction of travel.

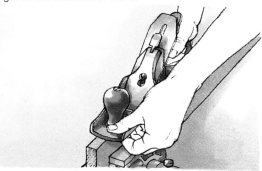

Planing edges

Maintain a square edge by putting pressure on the toe with your thumb, curling your fingers under the plane to act as a guide fence against the side of the work. Use a similar grip to hold the plane at an angle when planing chamfers along a workpiece.

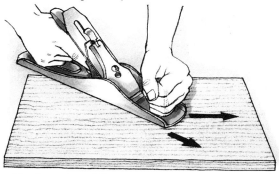

Planing a board flat

To plane a board flat, begin by planing at a slight angle across it from two directions. Check the surface with a straightedge (see page 15), then adjust the plane to take thinner shavings and finish with strokes parallel to the edges of the workpiece.

A woodworking blade is kept sharp by using abrasive whetstones to wear the metal to a narrow cutting edge. The better-quality natural stones are expensive, but you can get satisfactory results from cheaper synthetic stones. As part of the sharpening process, whetstones are lubricated with water or oil to make sure the steel does not overheat and to prevent fine particles of metal

and stone from clogging the abrasive surface. Generally, whetstones are sold as rectangular blocks—known as bench stones—for sharpening everyday tools, or as small knife-edge or teardrop-section stones for honing gouges and carving chisels. Blades can also be sharpened on a perfectly flat metal plate that has been dusted with abrasive powder.

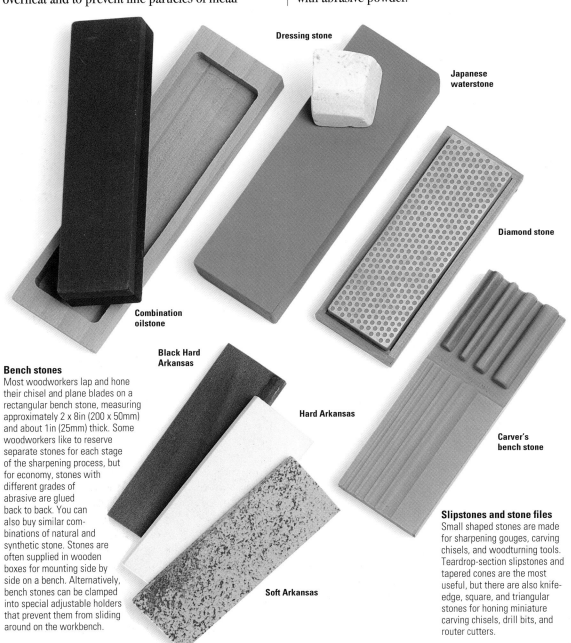

Dressing stone

Japanese waterstone

Diamond stone

Combination oilstone

Black Hard Arkansas

Hard Arkansas

Carver's bench stone

Soft Arkansas

Bench stones
Most woodworkers lap and hone their chisel and plane blades on a rectangular bench stone, measuring approximately 2 x 8in (200 x 50mm) and about 1in (25mm) thick. Some woodworkers like to reserve separate stones for each stage of the sharpening process, but for economy, stones with different grades of abrasive are glued back to back. You can also buy similar combinations of natural and synthetic stone. Stones are often supplied in wooden boxes for mounting side by side on a bench. Alternatively, bench stones can be clamped into special adjustable holders that prevent them from sliding around on the workbench.

Slipstones and stone files
Small shaped stones are made for sharpening gouges, carving chisels, and woodturning tools. Teardrop-section slipstones and tapered cones are the most useful, but there are also knife-edge, square, and triangular stones for honing miniature carving chisels, drill bits, and router cutters.

Oilstones

The majority of natural and man-made sharpening stones are lubricated with a light oil. Novaculite, generally considered to be the finest oilstone available, can be found only in Arkansas. This compact silica crystal occurs naturally in various grades. The coarse, mottled-gray Soft Arkansas stone removes metal quickly and is used for the preliminary shaping of edged tools. The white Hard Arkansas stone puts the honing angle on the cutting edge, which is then refined and polished with Black Arkansas stone. Even finer is the rare translucent variety.

Synthetic oilstones are made from sintered aluminum oxide or silicon carbide. Categorized as coarse, medium, and fine, man-made sharpening stones are far cheaper than their natural equivalents.

Waterstones

Because it is relatively soft and friable, a sharpening stone that is lubricated with water cuts faster than an equivalent oilstone: fresh abrasive particles are exposed and released constantly as a metal blade is rubbed across the surface of a waterstone. However, this soft bond also makes a waterstone vulnerable to accidental damage, especially when honing narrow chisels that could score the surface. Naturally occurring waterstones are so costly that most tool suppliers offer only synthetic varieties, which are almost as efficient.

Waterstones range from 800 grit at the coarse end, through 1000 and 1200 grits as medium grades, to something like 4000 to 6000 grits for final honing. Even finer, 8000-grit stones are available for polishing cutting edges. Extra-coarse 100 and 220 grits are used to repair damaged or very worn blades.

Chalklike dressing stones are rubbed across the face of wet finishing-grade stones to raise a slurry that improves their cutting action.

Grade	Synthetic oilstones	Natural oilstones	Waterstones
Coarse	Coarse	Soft Arkansas	800 grit
Medium	Medium	Hard Arkansas	1000–1200 grit
Fine	Fine	Black Hard Arkansas	4000–6000 grit
Extra-fine		Translucent Arkansas	8000 grit

Diamond stones

Extremely durable coarse- and fine-grade sharpening "stones" comprise a nickel-plated steel plate that is embedded with monocrystalline diamond particles and bonded to a rigid polycarbonate base. These fast-cutting sharpening tools, available as bench stones and narrow files, can be used dry or lubricated with water. Diamond stones will sharpen steel and carbide tools.

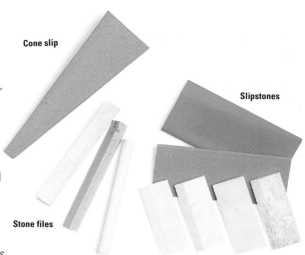

Cone slip

Slipstones

Stone files

Knife-edge slips

Metal lapping plates

Available as alternatives to conventional sharpening stones, oiled steel or cast-iron plates sprinkled with successively finer particles of silicon carbide produce an absolutely flat polished back to a plane or chisel blade and razor-sharp cutting edges. For the ultimate cutting edge on steel tools, finish with diamond-grit compound spread on a flat steel plate. Diamond abrasives are also used to hone carbide-tipped tools.

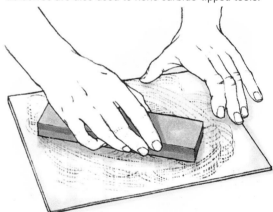

Caring for whetstones

Leave relatively coarse waterstones immersed in water for about five minutes before you use them; finer stones require less time. So that your waterstones are always ready for use, store them in vinyl boxes to prevent from moisture evaporating, keeping the temperature above freezing. Keep an oilstone covered to prevent dust from sticking to it, and clean the surface from time to time with solvent and a coarse cloth.

Eventually, all sharpening stones become concave through constant use. Flatten an oilstone by rubbing it on an oiled sheet of glass sprinkled with silicon-carbide powder. Regrind the surface of a waterstone on a sheet of 200-grit waterproof abrasive paper taped to glass.

SHARPENING BLADES

A new plane iron or chisel is ground at the factory with a 25-degree bevel across its width. Some woodworkers like to hone this bevel to a sharp edge for working softwood; but, because the edge would be too weak to stay sharp for long when cutting hardwoods, it is usual to hone a secondary bevel—the honing angle—on a whetstone. The exact angle depends on the tool and the type of work you intend to do with it. A bench plane, for example, works best with a honing angle of between 30 and 35 degrees. A paring chisel, which should never need driving through the wood with a mallet, can be honed to an angle as shallow as 20 degrees, but cutting a mortise in dense hardwood might merit a chisel with a cutting edge honed to 35 degrees.

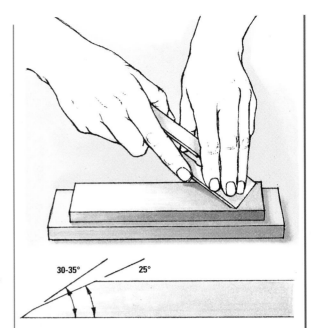

Lapping the back of a blade
Grinding a blade leaves minute scratches on the back and bevel, creating a serrated cutting edge that can never be truly sharp, even after honing. Consequently, the first stage of sharpening a new blade should be to flatten the back on a medium-grade bench stone or metal lapping plate.

Lubricate the stone and hold the blade flat on the surface, bevel side up. Rub the blade back and forth, maintaining pressure with your fingertips to prevent the blade from rocking. Concentrate on the 2in (50mm) of blade directly behind the cutting edge—the rest of the blade can be left with a factory finish. Repeat the process on a fine whetstone until the metal shines.

Honing a plane blade
Grasp the blade, bevel side down, with your index finger extended along one edge. Place the fingertips of your free hand on top of the blade, just behind the cutting edge.

Place the grinding bevel on a lubricated medium-grade bench stone, rocking the blade gently until you can feel the bevel is flat on the surface. Turn a wide blade to one side so the whole of the cutting edge is in contact with the stone.

Tilt the blade up onto its cutting edge and rub it back and forth along the entire length of the stone to hone the secondary angle. Keep your wrists firm, in order to maintain a constant angle.

Honing a chisel
Sharpen a chisel exactly as described above—but, because most chisel blades are relatively narrow, move the cutting edge from one side of the bench stone to the other while honing to avoid wearing a hollow down the middle.

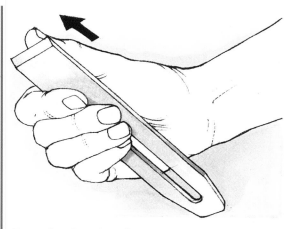

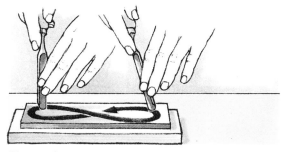

Sharpening an out-cannel gouge
To hone the edge of an out-cannel gouge (see page 29), rub the tool crosswise on a bench stone, describing a figure of eight stroke while rocking the blade from side to side. This brings the whole of the curved edge into contact with the stone and evens out the wear.

Removing the wire edge
Once you have honed a bevel about ⅓₂in (1mm) wide, continue with sharpening the plane blade or chisel on a fine-grade whetstone. Eventually the process wears a "wire edge" on the blade—a burr you can feel on the back of the blade with your thumb. Remove the burr by lapping the back of the blade on the fine stone, hone the bevel again with a few light strokes, and lap once more until the burr breaks off, leaving a sharp edge.

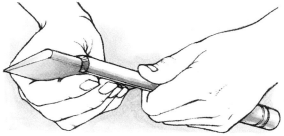

Stropping the blade
The final stage is to polish the cutting edge by honing it on an extra-fine stone (see page 37) or a leather strop—a strip of thick hide lubricated with a small cake of fine stropping paste.

Removing the burr and stropping
Remove the burr raised on the inside of the blade with a lubricated slipstone. Finally, wrap the stone with a strip of soft leather to strop the edge.

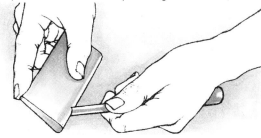

USING A HONING GUIDE
If you have trouble maintaining an accurate bevel when sharpening chisels and planes, try clamping the blade in a honing guide, a simple jig that holds it at the required angle to a whetstone. A honing guide, of which there are numerous different styles, is convenient for sharpening short spokeshave blades.

Honing an in-cannel gouge
Use a similar slipstone to hone the bevel on the concave edge of an in-cannel gouge.

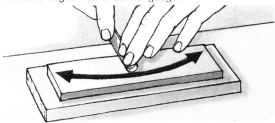

Removing the wire edge
Rub the back of an in-cannel gouge along a lubricated bench stone to remove the wire edge (see top left). Keep the back of the gouge flat on the stone while rocking the tool from side to side.

HAND DRILLS AND BRACES

Rugged but lightweight hand drills and ratchet braces are convenient for working on site since they are completely independent of any power source. A brace is especially useful for boring holes up to 2in (50mm) in diameter and can also be used to drive large screws.

1 Dowel bits
2 Countersink bit
3 Twist drills
4 Jennings-pattern auger bit
5 Solid-center auger bit
6 Expansive bits
7 Center bit
8 Screwdriver bit
9 Brace countersink bit

Hand drill

No longer featured in every woodworker's tool kit, the hand drill is nevertheless a beautifully engineered tool. Cranking the handle causes the chuck to rotate at relatively high speeds via a system of gear wheels. With some models the drive mechanism is encased in a cast-metal shell. The chuck will accommodate a wide range of twist drills and dowel bits.

Ratchet brace

Tool manufacturers still offer a variety of braces, including a special ratchet brace for boring holes through ceiling and floor joists, for plumbing and electrical wiring. An ordinary brace is driven by cranking its frame clockwise while pressure is applied to the round handle at the rear of the tool. The circle described by the moving frame is known as the sweep, and braces are listed in tool catalogs according to the diameter of their sweep. A 10in (250mm) brace is more or less standard.

A ratchet mechanism allows the tool to be used in confined spaces where a complete sweep is impossible; having cranked the handle as far as possible, the ratchet allows for movement in the opposite direction, leaving the chuck stationary until clockwise rotation is resumed. Operating a cam ring reverses the ratchet mechanism, so you can withdraw the drill bit.

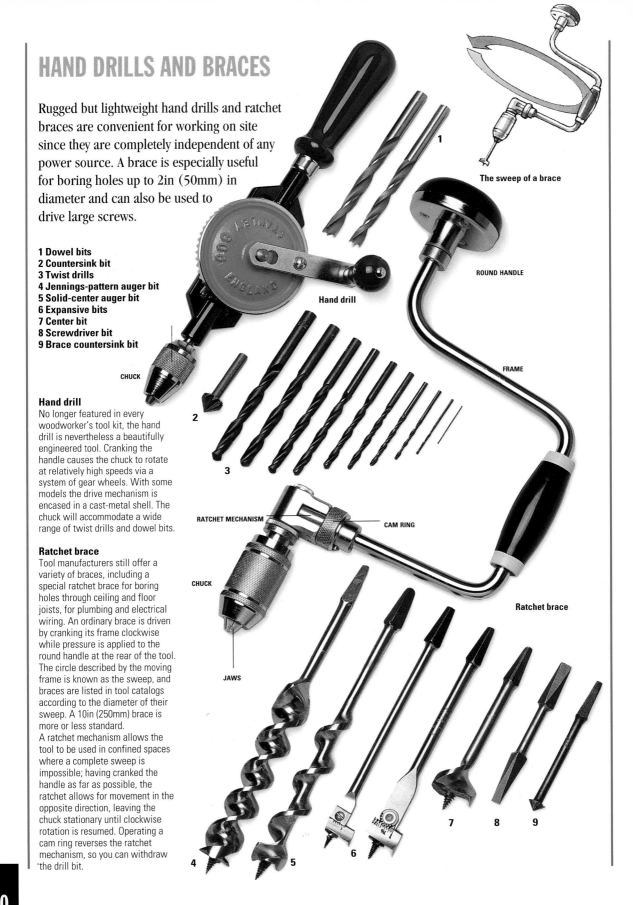

The sweep of a brace

ROUND HANDLE

FRAME

Hand drill

CHUCK

RATCHET MECHANISM

CAM RING

CHUCK

JAWS

Ratchet brace

40

Drill bits

The jaws of a hand drill take cylindrical twist drills and dowel bits. Braces are designed to accommodate special square-shanked bits, but some have universal jaws that will also accept cylindrical-shank drills.

Twist drills

Simple twist drills are made with a pair of helical flutes (twisted grooves) that clear the waste from the hole as the drill bores into the wood. The flutes culminate in two cutting edges that form a pointed tip to the drill. Most hand drills take bits up to a maximum diameter of ⅜in (9mm). Many woodworkers opt for a set of twist drills that will bore into metal as well as wood.

Dowel bits

These are wood-boring twist drills with sharp lead points that prevent them from wandering off line. Two sharp spurs per bit cut a clean-edged hole.

Auger bits

A solid-center auger bit for a ratchet brace has a single helical twist that brings the waste to the surface and serves to keep the bit on line when boring deep holes. It has a pair of spurs at the cutting tip that score the wood ahead of the cutting edges to make sure a crisp edge to the hole. The lead screw in the center pulls the bit into the wood. The similar Jennings-pattern auger bit has a double helical twist. Auger bits range from ¼ to 1½in (6 to 38mm) in diameter.

Expansive bits

An adjustable expansive bit will cut a hole of any size between limits. Depending on the model, an expansive bit is capable of cutting holes between ½ and 1½in (12 and 38mm) in diameter or, alternatively, between ⅞ and 3in (22 and 75mm).

Center bits

Since center bits are designed to bore relatively shallow holes, from 2¾ to 4½in (68 to 112mm) deep, they are simpler and therefore cheaper than the equivalent auger bits.

Screwdriver bits

A special double-ended bit converts a brace into a heavy-duty screwdriver.

Countersink bits

Countersink bits, whether for a hand drill or a brace, are used to cut tapered recesses in order to accommodate the heads of woodscrews so they lie flush with the surface of the work.

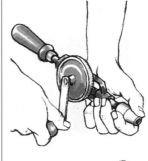

Operating a hand-drill chuck

To open the jaws of a hand drill, hold the chuck in one hand and crank the handle counterclockwise. Load a drill bit, grip the chuck and turn the handle clockwise to tighten the jaws.

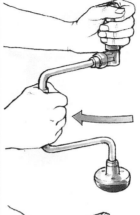

Fitting a bit into a ratchet brace

Lock the brace ratchet by centering the cam ring, then grip the chuck in one hand and turn the frame clockwise. Drop a bit into the chuck and reverse the action to close the jaws.

Using a hand drill

Place the tip of the drill bit on the work and gently move the handle back and forth until the bit begins to bite into the wood. Crank the handle at speed to bore a hole to the required depth. Don't apply too much pressure when using small twist drills; the weight of the tool alone will be enough to encourage the drill to penetrate the wood.

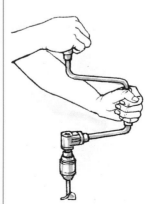

Boring with a brace

Hold the brace upright with one hand while cranking the frame with the other. To bore horizontally, steady the round handle against your body. To retrieve the bit, lock the ratchet and reverse the action a couple of turns to release the lead screw; then pull on the tool while moving the frame back and forth.

POWER DRILLS

A power drill is not only an invaluable woodworking tool—most people also own at least one mains-powered or cordless drill for household repairs and maintenance. Consequently, there is an immense choice of drills on the market, from cheap, virtually "throw-away" tools to durable and sophisticated drills for the professional builder and carpenter. Although a middle-of-the-line drill is adequate for woodworking, it makes sense to choose a tool that will satisfy all possible requirements.

Corded power drills
Most woodworkers continue to opt for a corded drill. They may be relatively heavy and bulky, but they are extremely tough and reliable tools that will run more or less continuously for hours on end, provided you have access to an electricity outlet.

Hammer action
Throwing a switch engages the drill's hammer action that delivers several hundred blows per second behind the drill bit to help break up masonry when boring into stone or brick walls. Hammer action is never needed for woodwork.

DEPTH STOP

HAMMER-ACTION SWITCH

SPEED SELECTION

KEYLESS CHUCK

BOSCH

CSB 550 RP

550 W · Beton Ø max. 15 mm

Electric drill

REVERSE-ACTION SWITCH

VARIABLE-SPEED TRIGGER

LOCK BUTTON

Drill chucks
Most chucks have three self-centering jaws that grip the shank of a drill bit. Some chucks need tightening with a special toothed key to make sure the drill bit is held securely by the jaws and will not slip in use, but a great many drills are made with "keyless" chucks that take a firm grip on the bit simply by turning a cylindrical collar that surrounds the mechanism.

Depth stop
An adjustable depth stop comes to rest against the work when the drill bit has bored to the required depth.

Reverse action
A reverse-action switch changes the direction of rotation so the power drill can be used to extract screws.

Trigger lock
Depressing a button on the drill's handle locks the trigger for continuous running. Squeezing the trigger again releases the lock button.

Speed selection
Although a few basic drills have a limited range of fixed speeds selected by operating a switch, the majority of drills are variable-speed tools, controlled by the amount of pressure applied to the trigger. On most models, it is also possible to select the maximum rotational speed by turning a small dial that limits the movement of the trigger. Many drills also incorporate electronic speed-control systems that maintain optimum speed when the load applied to the drill bit changes. A similar system will often protect the motor from damage if the bit jams in the work and may also minimize the initial jolt as the high-speed electric motor starts up. Manufacturers recommend a range of speeds at which their drills will perform best; however, as a rule of thumb, select a fast speed for boring into wood, but slower speeds for drilling metal and masonry and to drive in screws.

1

2

3

1 Countersink bit
2 Drill-and-countersink bit
3 Drill-and-counterbore bit
4 Plug cutter

4

Power-drill bits

Most power drills have a chuck capacity—the maximum size of drill-bit shank that the chuck will accommodate—of ⅜ or ½in (10 or 13mm). The shank size of a twist drill or dowel bit (see page 75) corresponds exactly to the size of hole that a particular bit will bore. However, a great many wood-boring bits are capable of making holes larger than their shank diameter.

Reduced-shank twist drills

Twist drills ½ to 1in (13 to 25mm) in diameter are made with reduced shanks that will fit a standard-size power-drill chuck. Twist drills are not easy to locate the dead center of a hole; when drilling hardwoods, in particular, it therefore pays to mark the center of a hole first, using a metalworking punch.

Spade bits

These are inexpensive drill bits made for power-drilling large holes from ¼ to 1½in (6 to 38mm) in diameter. A long lead point makes for positive location even when drilling at an angle to the face of the work.

Forstner bits

Forstner bits leave exceptionally clean flat-bottomed holes up to 2in (50mm) in diameter. Because the bit will not be deflected, even by wild grain or knots, you can bore overlapping holes and holes that run out to the edge of the work without difficulty.

Countersink bits

Similar to the countersink bits made for hand drills and braces (see page 41), these drill bits are used to make tapered recesses for the heads of wood screws. Center the bit on a clearance hole bored in the wood, and run the power drill at high speed for a clean finish.

Drill-and-countersink bits

These drill bits cut a pilot hole, clearance hole, and countersink for a wood screw in one operation. Each bit is matched to a particular size of screw.

Drill-and-counterbore bits

Instead of cutting a tapered recess for a screw head, this type of bit leaves a neat hole that allows the screw to be driven below the face of the workpiece.

Plug cutters

These cut cylindrical plugs of wood to hide the heads of counterbored woodscrews.

Screwdriver bits

Made to drive slotted and crosshead screws.

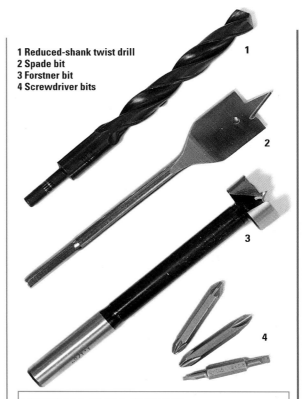

1 Reduced-shank twist drill
2 Spade bit
3 Forstner bit
4 Screwdriver bits

VERTICAL DRILL STANDS

A vertical stand converts a portable power drill into a serviceable drill press. Pulling on the spring-loaded feed lever lowers the drill bit into the wood: the depth of stopped holes can be preset, using a gauge on the stand. Bolt or screw the cast-metal base to a bench.

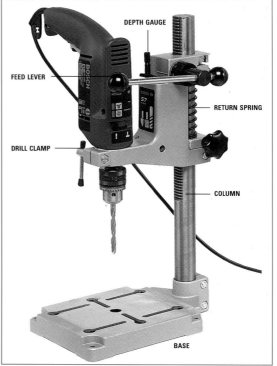

DEPTH GAUGE

FEED LEVER

RETURN SPRING

DRILL CLAMP

COLUMN

BASE

SCREWDRIVERS

Nowadays, many woodworkers use a power screwdriver or at least a large pump-action driver for any form of batch production involving a number of screw fixings. However, in reality you need no more than a handful of basic screwdrivers for driving simple straight-slot and crosshead screws.

Cabinet screwdriver
The standard, general-purpose woodworking screwdriver has a relatively large, oval-shape plastic or wooden grip that fits comfortably in the palm of the hand. The traditional flat tip may be ground from a cylindrical shaft or flared and then ground back to a tapered tip. The tip must fit the screw slot snugly, so it is worth investing in a range of screwdriver sizes.

Crosshead screwdriver
Traditional-pattern wood screws and modern, fast-action, double-helical screws are both made with cross-shape slots to improve the grip between the screwdriver tip and screw. The matching screwdrivers are made with pointed tips ground with four flutes.

Screwdriver bits
Straight-slot and crosshead bits are available for use with power screwdrivers or variable-speed electric drills.

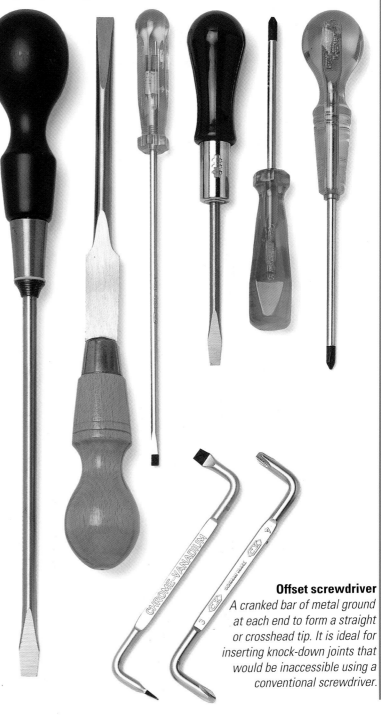

From left to right
Modern cabinet screwdriver
Traditional cabinet screwdriver
Fluted-handled screwdriver
Ratchet screwdriver
Posidriv screwdriver
Phillips screwdriver

Offset screwdriver
A cranked bar of metal ground at each end to form a straight or crosshead tip. It is ideal for inserting knock-down joints that would be inaccessible using a conventional screwdriver.

WOODWORKING CLAMPS

Interlocking woodworking joints are designed to insure optimum contact area between components so that they bond well with adhesive. A well-cut joint requires the minimum of clamping pressure, the main purpose of using clamps being to help assemble the workpiece and hold the parts together while the glue sets. It is always useful to have plenty of clamps available, but pairs of each type in a couple of sizes should suffice. Complete sets of clamps are relatively expensive, but you can acquire them over a period of time or rent them as required.

1 Pipe clamp
2 Bar clamp
3 Fast-action
 clamp
4 C-clamp
5 Long-reach
 C-clamp
6 Short fast-action
 clamp
7 Parallel clamp

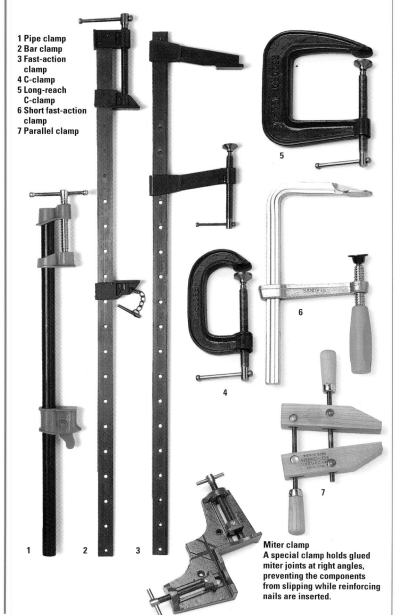

Miter clamp
A special clamp holds glued miter joints at right angles, preventing the components from slipping while reinforcing nails are inserted.

Fast-action clamps
Fast-action clamps are designed for speedy adjustment to fit the size of the work. Various versions are available. The bar type has two movable jaws, one of which is also screw-adjustable. On the smaller version of the clamp, only the screw-adjustable jaw is movable. A lightweight clamp has wooden jaws with a cam-action that provides clamping force.

Parallel clamps
A traditional clamp with wide wooden jaws that can be set to apply even pressure over a broad area. A parallel clamp is particularly useful when assembling out-of-square frames or for clamping tapered workpieces.

Bar clamps
Bar clamps are used for assembling large frames, panels, and carcasses. A bar clamp has a screw-adjustable jaw attached to one end of a flat steel bar. To accommodate assemblies of different sizes, a second movable jaw slides along the bar and is secured at the required position with a tapered steel pin, which passes behind the jaw into one of a series of holes in the bar. The clamps range from 1ft 6in to 4ft (450 to 1200mm) in length.

C-clamps
The C-clamp is an excellent general-purpose cramp that is often used to hold wood to a bench while you work on it. Usually made from cast iron, the frame forms a fixed jaw. Clamping force is applied by a screw, fitted with a ball-jointed shoe. C-clamps are manufactured in many sizes.

Pipe clamps
Similar in most respects to bar clamps, the jaws are attached to a length of round steel pipe.

WOODWORKING ADHESIVES

Supplied in liquid form, or as a powder or granules for mixing with water, woodworking glues can be applied with a brush, roller, or spreader. All adhesives are absorbed into the wood's cell structure, forming a strong link between the fibers of both halves of a joint; however, those that set by evaporation are rarely water-resistant. For a bond in moist conditions, select one that cures by chemical reaction.

APPLYING WOODWORKING GLUE

Joints should be made to fit well, rather than relying on the gap-filling properties of adhesive. Make sure the gluing surfaces are clean and free from grease. Some woods, such as teak and rosewood, are best glued as soon after cutting as possible, before their natural resins form a surface film that prevents glue from being absorbed properly.

Working in a warm, dry atmosphere, apply glue in a thin, even layer to both halves of a joint. Take care to coat the surfaces of a mortise, since most of the glue applied to the tenon is wiped off as the joint is assembled.

Don't rush when gluing up, but work as quickly as practicable, in order to assemble joints before the wood begins to swell and the glue starts to set. For a large or complicated assembly, use a two-part glue that is applied separately to joining surfaces. Place components in clamps (see page 94), and wipe off excess adhesive with a damp cloth.

PVA adhesive
Commonly known as white glue, polyvinyl-acetate (PVA) glue is a popular and convenient adhesive for joint-making. A ready-mixed emulsion supplied in plastic bottles, PVA sets by evaporation. It is a non-toxic glue that is easy to apply and is almost clear when set.

General-purpose PVA glue is only suitable for interior work. Although it forms a strong bond, the glue line remains relatively flexible and may creep (allow movement) when a joint is subjected to a prolonged heavy load. It does not sand well, as friction causes the glue to soften and clog abrasive paper.

Aliphatic-resin PVA glue is similar to the general-purpose version, but has improved moisture resistance and is less flexible.

Chemical-bonding, "cross-linking" PVA glue is even more water-resistant and forms an exceptionally strong bond.

Urea- and resorcinol-resin adhesives
Urea-formaldehyde-resin glue is a two-part adhesive that sets by chemical reaction. It is an excellent water-resistant adhesive that dries with a hard glue line. The resin and hardener are usually supplied pre-mixed as dry powders that are activated when mixed with water; the mixture remains workable for 20 minutes.

With some urea glues, the resin is packaged with a separate liquid hardener. The resin is applied to one half of the joint, the hardener to the other, and the glue only begins to set when the joint is assembled.

For even greater strength coupled with superior water-resistance, choose a resorcinol-formaldehyde glue, a two-part adhesive that is mixed prior to application. Either a liquid resin is supplied with a powdered hardener; or both constituents are in liquid form. Resorcinol resin dries to a reddish-brown glue line.

When working with uncured glue that contains formaldehyde, always work in a well-ventilated workshop, and wear a face mask, gloves, and eye protectors.

Hide glue
Traditional hide glue has been largely superseded by synthetic-resin adhesives, but still has advantages for furniture restoration and veneering. It is a strong-smelling, but non-toxic, glue made from animal skins and bone. It forms a strong bond that can be reversed by the application of heat and moisture. Hide glue is usually supplied in granular form for dissolving in water heated in a jacketed glue pot. When rendered to a smooth, runny consistency, the glue is applied hot to both joining surfaces. It sets, by cooling and evaporation, in about two hours.

THE NATURE OF
WOOD

THE ORIGINS OF WOOD

Trees, whether growing in forests or standing alone, not only help control our climate but also provide habitats for a vast number of plants and living creatures. Tree derivatives range from natural foodstuffs to extracts used in manufacturing products such as resins, rubber, and pharmaceuticals. When trees are cut down and converted into wood, they provide an infinitely adaptable and universally useful material.

What makes a tree?

Botanically, trees belong to the *Spermatophyta*—a division of seed-bearing plants which is subdivided into *Gymnospermae* and *Angiospermae*. The former are needle-leaved coniferous trees, known as softwoods, and the latter are broadleaved trees that may be deciduous or evergreen; they are known as hardwoods. All trees are perennials, which means they continue their growth for at least three years.

The main stem of a typical tree is known as a bole or trunk, and carries a crown of leaf-bearing branches. A root system both anchors the tree in the ground and absorbs water and minerals to sustain it. The outer layer of the trunk acts as a conduit to carry sap from the roots to the leaves.

Nutrients and photosynthesis

Trees take in carbon dioxide from the air through pores in the leaves called stomata, and evaporation from the leaves draws the sap through minute cells (see below). When the green pigment present in leaves absorbs energy from sunlight, organic compounds are made from carbon dioxide and water. This reaction, called photosynthesis, produces the nutrients on which a tree lives, and at the same time gives off oxygen into the atmosphere. The nutrient produced by the leaves is dispersed down through the tree to the growing parts, and is also stored by particular cells.

Although it is often thought that wood "breathes" and needs to be nourished as part of its maintenance, once a tree is felled, it dies. Any subsequent swelling or shrinking is simply a reaction of the wood to its environment as it absorbs and exudes moisture, in a similar way to a sponge. Wood finishes such as waxes and oils enhance and protect the surface, and to some extent help stabilize movement, but they do not "feed" the wood.

Cellular structure

A mass of cellulose tubular cells bond together with lignin, an organic chemical, to form the structure of wood. These cells provide support for the tree, circulation of sap, and food storage. They vary in size, shape, and distribution, but are generally long and thin, and run longitudinally with the main axis of the tree's trunk or branches. The orientation produces characteristics relating to the direction of grain, and the varying size and distribution of cells between species produce the character of wood textures, from fine to coarse.

Identifying wood

Examination of cells enables the identification of cut wood as being a softwood or hardwood. The simple cell structure of softwoods is composed mainly of tracheid cells, which provide initial sap conduction and physical support. They form regular radiating rows and make up the main body of the tree.

Hardwoods have fewer tracheids than softwoods; instead, they have vessels or pores that conduct sap and fibers that give support.

Mature montane coniferous forest

Carbon dioxide
Drawn in from the
air through leaves.

Oxygen
Given out into the
air by living trees.

Leaf-bearing branches
Leaves produce nutrients
that feed the tree
by photosynthesis.

Trunk
The trunk supports
the leaf-bearing branches
and is the main source
of useful wood.

**Gymnosperms—
needle-leaved trees**

**Angiosperms—
broadleaved trees**

Root system
Roots anchor the tree
and absorb moisture
and minerals from the soil.

HOW TREES GROW

A thin layer of living cells between the bark and the wood, called the cambium, subdivides every year to form new wood on the inner side and phloem or bast on the outside. As the inner girth of the tree increases, the old bark splits and new bark is formed by the bast. Cambial cells are weak and thin-walled; in the growing season, when they are moisture-laden, the bark can be easily peeled. In winter months, the cells stiffen and bind the bark firmly. The new wood cells on the inside develop into two specialized types: living cells that store food for the tree, and non-living cells that conduct sap up the tree and provide support for it. These two types make up the sapwood layer.

Each year, a new ring of sapwood is built up on the outside of the previous year's growth. At the same time, the oldest sapwood nearer the center is no longer used to conduct water; it is chemically converted into the heartwood that forms the structural spine of the tree. The area of heartwood increases annually, while the sapwood remains at around the same thickness during the tree's life.

Bark
The outer protective layer of dead cells. The term "bark" can also include the living inner tissue.

Bast or phloem
The inner bark tissue that conducts synthesized food.

European oak
Quercus petraea
The photograph shows a cross section of a European oak trunk.

Cambium layer
The thin layer of living cell tissue that forms new wood and bark.

Sapwood
The new wood, the cells of which conduct or store nutrients.

Annual-growth ring
The layer of wood formed in one growing period, made up of large earlywood and small latewood cells.

Ray cells
Radiating sheets of cells that conduct nutrients horizontally; also called "medullary rays".

Heartwood
The mature wood that forms the tree's spine.

Pith
The central core of cells. This can be weak and often suffers from fungal and insect attack.

Ray cells

Ray cells, or medullary cells, radiate from the center of the tree. They carry and store nutrients horizontally through the sapwood, in the same way as the cells that follow the axis of the trunk. The flat vertical bands formed by ray cells can hardly be detected in softwoods; in some hardwoods such as oak, particularly when it is quarter-sawn, the ray cells are plainly visible.

Sapwood

Sapwood can usually be recognized by its lighter color, which contrasts with the darker heartwood. However, this difference is less distinct on light-colored woods, particularly softwoods. Because sapwood cells are relatively thin-walled and porous, they tend to give up moisture quickly and shrink more than the denser heartwood. Conversely, this porosity means that sapwood can readily absorb stains and preservatives.

For the woodworker, sapwood is inferior to heartwood; furniture makers usually cut it to waste. It is not very resistant to fungal decay, and the carbohydrates stored in some cells are also liable to insect attack.

Heartwood

The dead sapwood cells that form heartwood have no further part in the tree's growth and can become blocked with organic material. Hardwoods with blocked cells—white oak, for instance—are impervious and much better suited to tasks such as tight cooperage than woods like red oak, which have open heartwood cells and are thus relatively porous.

The chemical substances that cause the dead cell walls to change color, sometimes deeply in the case of hardwoods, are called extractives. They also provide some resistance to insect and fungal attack.

Annual rings

The distinct banding made by earlywood and latewood corresponds to one season's growth and means the age of a felled tree, and the climatic conditions through which it has grown, can be determined. In the simplest example, wide annual rings indicate good growing conditions, narrow ones poor or drought conditions, but study of the annual rings can tell the history of the tree's growth in detail.

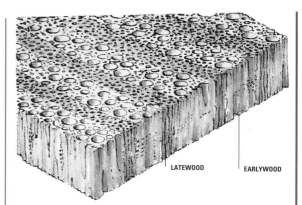

LATEWOOD   EARLYWOOD

Earlywood

Earlywood, or springwood, is the rapid part of the annual-growth ring that is laid down in spring, at the early part of the growing season. In softwood, thin-walled tracheid cells form the bulk of the earlywood and facilitate the rapid conduction of sap. In hardwood, open tubelike vessels perform the same function. Earlywood can usually be recognized as the wider band or paler-colored wood in each growth ring.

Latewood

Latewood, or summerwood, grows more slowly in the summertime, and produces thicker-walled cells. Their slower growth creates harder and usually darker wood, which is less able to conduct sap but provides support to the tree.

Young hardwood forest

SELECTING WOOD

The selection of a suitable wood for a project is usually based on the appearance of the material and its physical and working properties. When the species has been selected, the boards, ideally from the same tree, are then chosen for quality and condition. Then the wood is evaluated at the making stage, in order to explore its full potential in the finished work.

Buying wood

Lumber suppliers usually stock the softwoods most commonly used for carpentry and cabinetmaking—spruce, fir, and pine. They are generally sold as "dimension" or "dressed" stock, the trade terms for sawn or surface-planed sections cut to standard sizes. One or more of the faces may be surfaced.

Most hardwoods are sold as boards of random width and length, although some species can be bought as dimension stock. Dimension lumber is sold in 1ft or 300mm units (see right); check which system your supplier uses, as the metric unit is about 5mm (³⁄₁₆in) shorter than a foot. Whichever system you use, always allow extra length for waste and selection.

When working out lumber requirements, remember that planing processes can remove at least ⅛in (3mm) from each face of the wood, making the actual width and thickness less than the "nominal" or "sawn size" quoted by the lumberyard. The length, however, is always as quoted.

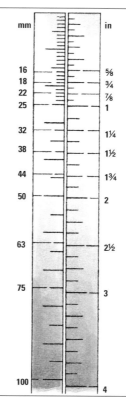

STANDARD AND METRIC MEASUREMENTS

The lumber trade is an international business, in which the producer countries use either the standard or metric systems of measurement. Though there are moves for unification toward the metric system, both are in use at time of writing. To avoid confusion and inaccuracies, only one system should be used when specifying dimensions. This actual-size bar chart shows the slight variation for standard sizes up to 4in (100mm).

Grading woods

Softwoods are graded for evenness of grain and the amount of allowable defects, such as knots. For general woodworking, better-quality "appearance" and "non-stress" grades are probably the most useful. Stress-graded softwoods are rated for structural use where strength is important. The trade term "clear timber" is used for knot-free or defect-free wood, but is not usually available from suppliers unless specified.

Hardwoods are graded by the area of defect-free wood: the greater the area, the higher the grade. The most suitable grades for general woodworking are firsts and seconds.

Although specialized firms supply wood by mail order, personal selection is by far the best option. Take a block plane with you when buying lumber, so you can expose a small area of wood if the color and grain are obscured by dirt or saw marks.

Cutting lists

Cutting lists are used to specify the finished length, width, and thickness of every component of a project. The list should also state the material and quantity required. A cutting list means the lumberyard can supply the material in the most economic way, and provides the woodworker with a schedule for converting the wood to size.

Stacks of boards at a timber yard

Defects in wood

If wood is not dried carefully, stresses can mar it or make it difficult to work. Insufficient drying can cause shrinkage of dimensioned parts, joints opening, warping, and splitting. Check the surface for obvious faults, such as splits, knots, and uneven grain. Look at the end section, to identify how the wood was cut from the log and to spot any distortion. Sight along the length to test for twisting or bowing. Ingrained stains, caused by water collecting in the stack or the use of incompatible wood for the stickers, can be difficult to remove, so check for sticker marks. In addition, look for evidence of insect attack or traces of fungal growth.

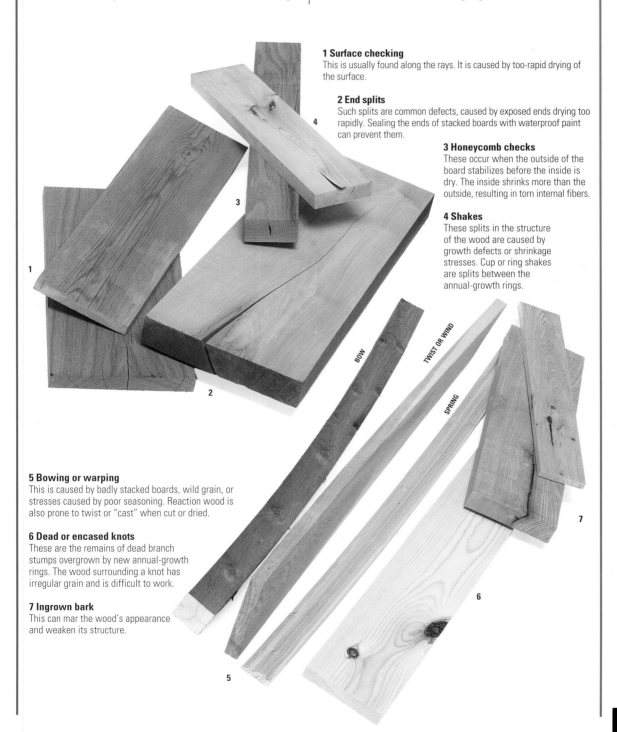

1 Surface checking
This is usually found along the rays. It is caused by too-rapid drying of the surface.

2 End splits
Such splits are common defects, caused by exposed ends drying too rapidly. Sealing the ends of stacked boards with waterproof paint can prevent them.

3 Honeycomb checks
These occur when the outside of the board stabilizes before the inside is dry. The inside shrinks more than the outside, resulting in torn internal fibers.

4 Shakes
These splits in the structure of the wood are caused by growth defects or shrinkage stresses. Cup or ring shakes are splits between the annual-growth rings.

5 Bowing or warping
This is caused by badly stacked boards, wild grain, or stresses caused by poor seasoning. Reaction wood is also prone to twist or "cast" when cut or dried.

6 Dead or encased knots
These are the remains of dead branch stumps overgrown by new annual-growth rings. The wood surrounding a knot has irregular grain and is difficult to work.

7 Ingrown bark
This can mar the wood's appearance and weaken its structure.

PROPERTIES OF WOOD

In many woodworking projects, the grain pattern, color, and texture are the most important factors when choosing which woods to work. Though equally important, the strength and working characteristics are often a secondary consideration —and when using veneer, the appearance is all.

Working wood is a constant process of discovery and learning. Each piece is unique, and any section of wood taken from the same tree, even from the same board, will be different and a challenge to the woodworker's skills. You can only gain a full understanding of wood's properties by working it and experiencing the way it behaves.

Grain

The mass of the wood's cell structure constitutes the grain of the wood, which follows the main axis of the tree's trunk. The disposition and degree of orientation of the longitudinal cells create different types of grain.

Trees that grow straight and even produce straight-grained wood. When cells deviate from the main axis of the tree, they produce cross-grained wood. Spiral grain comes from trees that twist as they grow; when this spiral growth changes direction from one angle to another, each change taking place over a few annual-growth rings, the result is interlocked grain. Wavy grain, which has short, even waves, and irregular curly grain occur in trees with an undulating cell structure. Wild grain is created when the cells change direction throughout the wood; irregular-grained woods of this kind can be difficult to work.

Random and undulating grain make various patterns in wood, according to the angle to the surface and light reflectivity of the cell structure. Boards with these configurations are particularly valued for veneer.

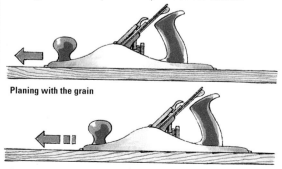

Planing with the grain

Planing against the grain

Working wood

Planing with the grain follows the direction of the grain where the fibers are parallel or slope up and away from the direction of the cutting action, resulting in smooth, trouble-free cuts. Planing a surface against the grain refers to cuts made where the fibers slope up and toward the direction of the planing action; this produces a rough cut. Sawing with the grain means cutting along the length of the wood in the same direction as the longitudinal cells. Sawing or planing across the grain describes cuts made more or less perpendicular to the grain of the wood.

Figure

The term grain is also used to describe the appearance of wood; however, what is really being referred to is a combination of natural features collectively known as the figure. These features include the difference in growth between the earlywood and latewood; the way color is distributed; the density, concentricity, or eccentricity of the annual-growth rings; the effect of disease or damage; and how the wood is converted.

Using figure

When tree trunks are tangentially cut, the plain-sawn boards display a U-shape pattern. When the trunk is radially cut or quarter-sawn, the series of parallel lines usually produces a less distinctive pattern.

The fork where the main stem of the tree and a branch meet provides curl, or crotch, figure that is sought-after for veneer. Burl wood, an abnormal growth on the side of a tree caused by injury, is used for veneer. It is popular among woodturners, as is the random-grain figure of stumpwood, from the base of the trunk or roots.

Texture

Texture refers to the relative size of the wood's cells. Fine-textured woods have small, closely spaced cells, while coarse-textured woods have relatively large cells. Texture also denotes the distribution of the cells in relation to the annual-growth rings. A wood where the difference between earlywood and latewood is marked has an uneven texture; one with only slight contrast in the growth rings is even-textured.

Coarse-textured woods, such as oak or ash, tend to have finer cells when they are slow-grown, and are also lighter and softer than when fast-grown. Fast-grown trees usually produce a more distinctive figure and harder, stronger, and heavier wood.

Effects of texture

The difference in texture between earlywood and latewood is important to the woodworker, as lighter-weight earlywood is easier to cut than the denser latewood. If tool-cutting edges are kept sharp, this should minimize any problems, but latewood can be left proud of the earlywood when finished with a power sander. Those woods with even-textured growth rings are generally the easiest to work and finish.

Ring-porous wood

Diffuse-porous wood

Hardwood porosity
The distribution of hardwood cells can have a marked effect on wood texture. The ring-porous hardwoods, such as oak or ash, have clearly defined rings of large vessels in the earlywood, and dense fibers and cell tissue in the latewood; this makes them more difficult to finish than the diffuse-porous woods, such as beech, where the vessels and fibers are relatively evenly distributed. Woods like mahogany can be diffuse-porous, but their larger cells can make them more coarse-textured.

Durability

Durability refers to a wood's performance when it is in contact with soil. Perishable wood is rated at less than 5 years, very durable at more than 25 years. The durability of a species can vary according to the level of exposure and climatic conditions.

Botanical classification

Although most woodworkers and lumberyards refer to woods by their common names, such as beech or walnut, the botanical name is the only universal term which can be relied upon to accurately identify a species of wood. In suppliers' catalogs and reference books, the terms "sp." or "spp." are commonly used to indicate that a wood may be one of a variety of species within a genus, or family of trees.

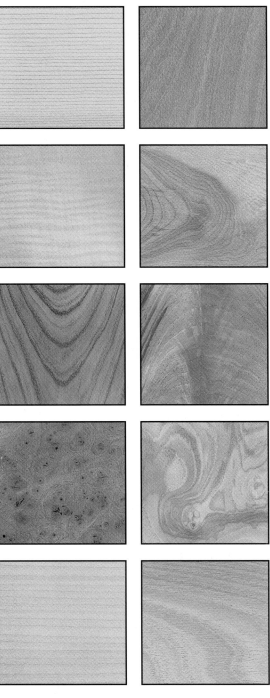

**Textures and patterns
(from left to right, in sequence):**

Straight grain (sitka spruce)	Spiral grain (satinwood)
Wavy grain (fiddleback sycamore)	Wild grain (yellow birch)
U-shape pattern (blackwood)	Curl or crotch (walnut)
Burl wood (elm)	Stumpwood (ash)
Fine-textured (linden)	Coarse-textured (sweet chestnut)

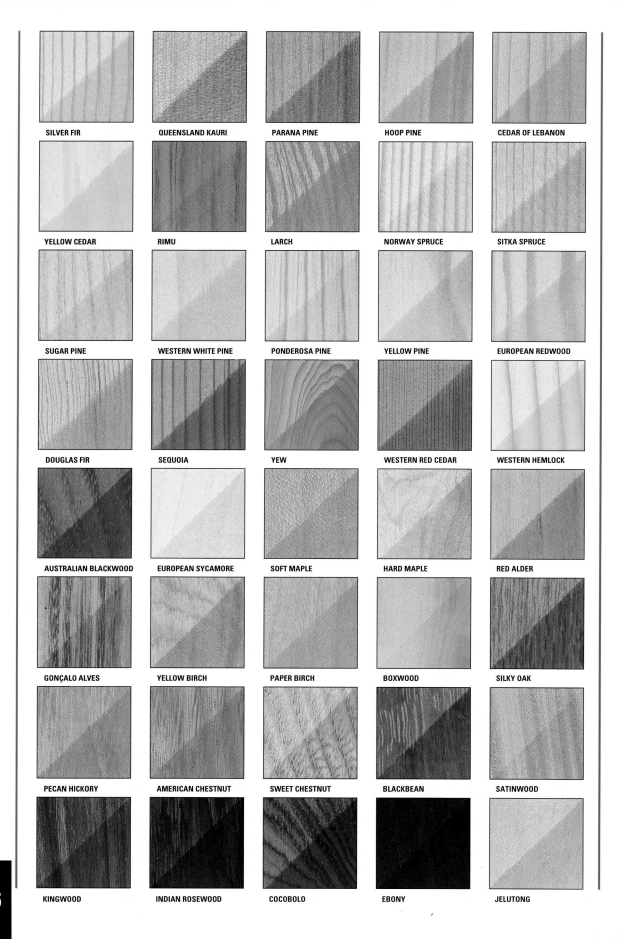

SILVER FIR	QUEENSLAND KAURI	PARANA PINE	HOOP PINE	CEDAR OF LEBANON
YELLOW CEDAR	RIMU	LARCH	NORWAY SPRUCE	SITKA SPRUCE
SUGAR PINE	WESTERN WHITE PINE	PONDEROSA PINE	YELLOW PINE	EUROPEAN REDWOOD
DOUGLAS FIR	SEQUOIA	YEW	WESTERN RED CEDAR	WESTERN HEMLOCK
AUSTRALIAN BLACKWOOD	EUROPEAN SYCAMORE	SOFT MAPLE	HARD MAPLE	RED ALDER
GONÇALO ALVES	YELLOW BIRCH	PAPER BIRCH	BOXWOOD	SILKY OAK
PECAN HICKORY	AMERICAN CHESTNUT	SWEET CHESTNUT	BLACKBEAN	SATINWOOD
KINGWOOD	INDIAN ROSEWOOD	COCOBOLO	EBONY	JELUTONG

QUEENSLAND WALNUT

UTILE

JARRAH

AMERICAN BEECH

It is the nature of wood to be varied in color, figure and texture. Even when wood is prepared and finished, it will continue to respond to its environment; not only will it "move", but the color will also alter in time by becoming lighter or darker, according to species. The result of this process is known as patina.

EUROPEAN BEECH

AMERICAN WHITE ASH

EUROPEAN ASH

RAMIN

LIGNUM VITAE

BUBINGA

BRAZILWOOD

BUTTERNUT

Color change
The most dramatic changes in color occur when a finish is applied; even a clear finish enriches and slightly darkens natural colors. The softwoods and hardwoods illustrated here are actual-size samples, illustrating the wood before and after the application of a clear surface finish.

AMERICAN WALNUT

EUROPEAN WALNUT

AMERICAN WHITEWOOD

BALSA

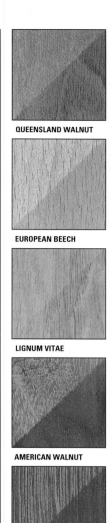

PURPLEHEART

AFRORMOSIA

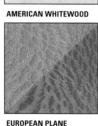

EUROPEAN PLANE

AMERICAN SYCAMORE

AMERICAN CHERRY

AFRICAN PADAUK

AMERICAN WHITE OAK

JAPANESE OAK

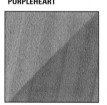

AMERICAN RED OAK

RED LAUAN

BRAZILIAN MAHOGANY

TEAK

EUROPEAN OAK

LIME

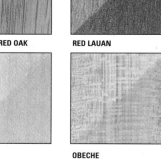

OBECHE

AMERICAN WHITE ELM

DUTCH & ENGLISH ELM

BASSWOOD

THE VERSATILITY OF WOOD

The uses to which wood can be put seem endless. So common has it become in our everyday environment that it is often taken for granted and hardly recognized for its value. The diversity of woods, with their variety of properties, provides a wide selection for the woodworker. However, the wonder of wood is not just in its availability or variety; its workability with even the simplest of hand tools has elevated it to the most-used raw material of all.

With the development of edged tools, the human species has been able to fashion wood to change and enhance its environment—one only has to look at the history of all cultures to see examples of wooden artefacts and structures. Even with the development of synthetic materials and the progress of automated, mechanized production of wood and wood products, the raw material is still processed by traditional methods to meet a neverending demand for products made from this most desirable natural material.

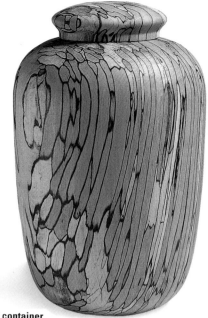

Lidded container
Spalted wood, which is caused by fungal attack, is much prized by woodturners for its incredible decorative patterns. In this example, the black "zone lines" and mottled coloring that penetrate the wood produce a unique random design that is exploited by the woodturner.

Ship frames
Oak has long been used in traditional building construction and shipbuilding. Here, massive curved-oak frames are fitted to a keel to construct a replica of John Cabot's ship, the *Matthew*; the original crossed the Atlantic in 1497.

Windsor chair

Typically made of turned spindles, steam-bent bows, and solid, shaped seats, traditional Windsor chairs are classic examples of the chairmaker's art. They are made in various regional styles, using native woods—such as ash, elm, yew, oak, beech, birch, maple, or poplar—and can be found, in original or reproduced forms, in homes around the world.

Seal table

The natural color and texture of a "found" piece of European-sycamore log are creatively transformed into this delightful carved seal. The wood also forms the base for a clear-glass table top that represents the surface of water.

Burl bowl

Solid burl wood is a favorite material for woodturners. In this striking example, the natural contours and textures of elm burr are accentuated by flaming the workpiece with a blowtorch during turning; the turned grooves and smooth inner surface add textural contrast.

Shaker box

The simple design and fine craftsmanship of the American Shaker sect are clearly seen in this handmade traditional oval box. Thin-cut cherry wood is steamed and bent around a form before the projecting "fingers" are secured with copper rivets; solid-wood ovals are then pinned into the lid and body.

PLYWOOD

Plywood is made from thin laminated sheets of wood called construction veneers, plys, or laminates. These are bonded at 90 degrees to each other, to form a strong, stable board; odd numbers of layers are used, to make sure that the grain runs the same way on the top and bottom.

Manufacturing plywood
A wide range of species of both hardwoods and softwoods is used to produce plywood. The veneers may be cut by slicing or rotary cutting—for softwoods, the latter is the most common method.

A debarked log is converted into a continuous sheet of veneer of a thickness between 1/16 and 1/4in (1.5 and 6mm). The sheet is clipped to size, then sorted and dried under controlled conditions before being graded into face, or core, plys. Defective plys are plugged and narrow core plies are stitched or spot-glued together before laminating.

The prepared sheets are laid in a glued "sandwich", the number depending on the type and thickness of plywood required, and hot-pressed. The boards are then trimmed to size and are usually sanded to fine tolerances on both sides.

Stocks of silver birch for plywood manufacture

STANDARD SIZES
Plywood is available in a wide range of sizes. The thickness of most commercially available plywood ranges from 1/8in (3mm) up to 1 3/16in (30mm), in increments of approximately 1/8in (3mm). Thinner "aircraft" plywood is available from specialized suppliers.

A typical board is 4ft (1.22m) wide, and boards 5ft (1.52m) wide are also available. The most common length is 8ft (2.44m), although boards up to 12ft (3.66m) can be purchased.

The grain of the face ply usually, but not always, follows the longest dimension of the board. It runs parallel to the first dimension quoted by the manufacturer, so a 4 x 8ft (1.22 x 2.44m) board will have the grain running across the width.

Plywood construction
Solid wood is a relatively unstable material, and a board will shrink or swell more across the fibers than it will along them. There is also a high risk of distortion, depending on how the board has been cut from the tree. The tensile strength of wood is greatest following the direction of the fibers, but wood will also readily split with the grain.

In order to counter this natural movement of wood, plywood is constructed with the fibers or grain of alternate plys set at right angles to one another, thus producing a stable, warp-resisting board with no natural direction of cleavage. The greatest strength of a panel is usually parallel to the face grain.

Plys
Most plywood is made with an odd number of plys to give a balanced construction, from three up; the number varies according to the thickness of the plys and the finished board. However many plys are used, the construction must be symmetrical about the center ply or the center line of the panel thickness.

The surface veneers of a typical plywood board are known as face plys. Where the quality of one ply is better than the other, the better ply is called the face and the other the back. The quality of the face plys is usually specified by a grading letter code (see opposite).

The plys that are immediately beneath, and laid perpendicular to, the face plys are known as cross-plys. The center ply (or plys) is known as the core.

USES OF PLYWOOD

The performance of plywood is determined not only by the quality of the plys, but also by the type of adhesive used in its manufacture. Major manufacturers test their products rigorously by taking batch samples through a series of tests that exceed service requirements. The glue bond of exterior grades is stronger than the wood itself, and panels made with formaldehyde glues must comply with a formaldehyde-emissions standard. Plywoods can be broadly grouped by usage.

Interior plywood (INT)

These plywoods are used for interior non-structural applications. They are generally produced with an appearance-grade face ply and poorer quality ply for the back. They are manufactured with light-colored urea-formaldehyde adhesive. Most are suitable for use in dry conditions, such as for furniture or wall paneling. The modified adhesive used in some boards affords them some moisture resistance, thus enabling them to be used in areas of high humidity. INT-grade plywood must not be used for exterior applications.

Exterior plywood (EXT)

Depending on the quality of the adhesive, EXT-grade plywoods can be used for fully or semi-exposed conditions, where structural performance is not required. They are often used for kitchen units or applications around showers and in bathrooms.

Boards suitable for fully exposed conditions are bonded with dark-colored phenol-formaldehyde (phenolic) adhesive. This type produces weather-and-boil-proof (WBP) plywood. WBP adhesives are those that comply with an established and tested standard and have proved to be highly resistant to weather, microorganisms, cold and boiling water, steam and dry heat over many years. Exterior-grade plywoods are also produced using melamine urea-formaldehyde adhesive. These boards are semi-durable under exposed conditions.

Marine plywood

Marine plywood is a high-quality, face-graded structural plywood, constructed from selected plys within a limited range of mahogany-type woods. It has no "voids" or gaps, and is bonded with a durable phenolic-resin adhesive. It is primarily produced for marine use, and can be used for interior units where water or steam may be present.

APPEARANCE GRADING

Plywood producers use a coding system to grade the appearance quality of the face plys used for boards. The letters do not refer to structural performance. Typical systems for softwood boards use the letters A, B, C, C plugged, and D.

The A grade is the best quality, being smooth-cut and virtually defect-free; D grade is the poorest, and has the maximum amount of permitted defects, such as knots, holes, splits, and discoloration. A-A grade plywood has two good faces, while a board classified as B-C has poorer-grade outer plys, with the better B grade used for the face and the C grade for the back.

Decorative plywoods are faced with selected matched veneers and are referred to by the wood species of the face veneer.

1 Trademark
The grading authority. Here, the American Plywood Association.

2 Panel grade
Identifies the grades of the face and back veneers.

3 Mill number
Code number of the producing mill.

4 Species group number
Group 1 is the strongest species.

5 Exposure classification
Indicates bond durability.

6 Product Standard number
Indicates the board meets the U.S. Product Standard.

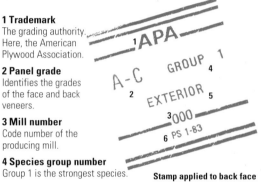

Stamp applied to back face

Stamp applied to edge

A-B · G-1 · EXT-APA · 000 · PS1-83

Typical grading stamps

Boards with A-grade or B-grade veneer on one side only are usually stamped on the back; those with A or B grades on both faces are usually stamped on the panel edge.

Structural plywood

Structural or engineering-grade plywood is produced for applications where strength and durability are the prime considerations. It is bonded with phenolic adhesive. A lower appearance-grade face ply is used, and boards may not have been sanded.

BLOCKBOARD AND LAMINBOARD

Blockboard is a form of plywood, by virtue of having a laminated construction. Where it differs from conventional plywood is in having its core constructed from strips of softwood cut approximately square in section; these are edge-butted but not glued. The core is faced with one or two layers of ply on each side.

Laminboard is similar to blockboard, but the core is constructed with narrow strips of softwood, each about $\frac{3}{16}$in (5mm) thick; these are usually glued together. Like blockboard, laminboard is made in both three- and five-ply construction. Its higher adhesive content makes laminboard denser and heavier than blockboard.

Laminboard
Because the core is less likely to "telegraph" or show through, this is superior to blockboard for veneer work. It is also more expensive. Boards of three- and five-ply construction are produced. With the latter, each pair of thin outer plies may run perpendicular to the core. Alternatively, the face ply only may run in line with the core strips.

Blockboard
This stiff material is suitable for furniture applications, particularly shelving and countertops. It makes a good substrate for veneer work, although the core strips can telegraph. It is made in similar panel sizes to plywood, with thicknesses ranging from $\frac{1}{2}$in (12mm) to 1in (25mm). Boards of three-ply construction are made up to 1$\frac{3}{4}$in (44mm) thick.

Laminboard   Blockboard

FIBERBOARDS

Fiberboards are made from wood that has been broken down to its basic fiber elements and reconstituted to make a stable, homogeneous material. Boards of various density are produced according to the pressure applied and the adhesive used in the manufacturing process.

Top to bottom:
Oak-veneered; medium-density fibrerboard; low-density board; high-density board.

Top to bottom:
Perforated pegboard, decorative-face hardboard, embossed hardboard, tempered hardboard, standard hardboard.

Grades of fiberboard

Most boards are made by forming wet fibers into a mat and bonding them, generally using the wood's natural resins, to produce boards of varying density.

Medium-density fiberboard (MDF)
This is manufactured using a dry process, in which synthetic resin bonds the fibers together, to produce greater strength. MDF is smooth on both faces and uniform in structure; it has a fine texture. It can be worked like wood and used as a substitute for solid wood in some applications, such as furniture-making. It can be cleanly profile-machined on the edges and faces, but does not accept screws well on its edges, which are likely to split; although stable, it swells when moist. Waterproof board is made for use in damp conditions. Boards are made in thicknesses of ¼ to 1¼in (6 to 32mm) and in a wide range of sizes. They make an excellent groundwork for veneer, and take paint finishes well.

Low-density (LM) board
This relatively soft board, usually ¼ to ½in (6 to 12mm) thick is used for pinboard or wall paneling.

High-density (HM) board
Heavier and stiffer than LM board, this is used for interior paneling applications.

Hardboards
Hardboard is a fiberboard that is manufactured in a similar way to LM and HM boards, but at higher pressures and temperatures.

Standard hardboard
This has one smooth and one textured face, and is made in a range of thicknesses, commonly from ⅛ to ¼in (3 to 6mm) in a wide range of panel sizes. It is an inexpensive material, commonly used for drawer bottoms and cabinet backs.

Duo-faced hardboard
Made from the same material as standard board, this has two smooth faces. It is used where both faces are likely to be seen, such as a panel of a framed door or cabinet.

Decorative hardboard
This is available as perforated, molded, or lacquered boards. Perforated types are used for screens, most others for wall paneling.

Tempered hardboard
Standard hardboard is impregnated with resin and oil to produce a stronger material that is water- and abrasion-resistant.

STORING BOARDS

To save space, man-made boards should be stored on their edges. A rack will keep the edges clear of the floor and support the boards evenly at a slight angle; to prevent a thin board from bending, support it from beneath with a thicker board.

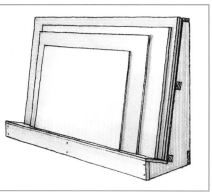

PARTICLE BOARDS

Wood-particle boards are made from small chips or flakes of wood bonded together under pressure—softwoods are generally used, although a proportion of hardwoods may be included. Various types of boards are produced according to the shape and size of the particles, their distribution through the thickness of the board, and the adhesive used to bind them together.

Manufacturing particle boards

The production of particle boards is a highly controlled automated process. The wood is converted into particles of the required size by chipping machines. After drying, the particles are sprayed with resin binders and spread to the required thickness with their grain following the same direction. This "mat" is hot-pressed under high pressure to the required thickness and then cured. The cooled boards are trimmed to size and sanded.

Working features

Particle boards are stable and uniformly consistent. Those constructed with fine particles have featureless surfaces and are highly suited as groundwork for home veneering. Decorative boards, preveneered with wood, paper foil, or plastic laminates, are also available. Most particle boards are relatively brittle and have a much lower tensile strength than plywood boards.

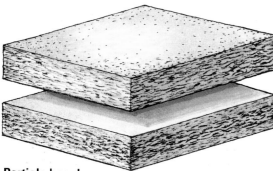

Particle board

The types of particle board most used by woodworkers are those of interior quality. Like other wood products, interior-grade particleboard is adversely affected by excess moisture—the board swells in its thickness and does not return to shape on drying. Moisture-resistant types, suitable for flooring or wet conditions, are available, and are used extensively in the building-construction trade.

Single-layer particle board
Made from a mat of similar-size, evenly distributed particles, this board has a relatively coarse surface suitable for wood veneer or plastic laminate, but not for painting.

Three-layer particle board
This board has a core layer of coarse particles sandwiched between two outer layers of fine high-density particles. The high proportion of resin in the outer layers produces a smooth surface that is suitable for most finishes.

Graded-density particle board
This board is a blend of coarse and very fine particles. Unlike three-layer particle board, there is a gradual transition from the coarse interior through to the fine surface.

Decorative particle board
These boards are faced with selected wood veneers, plastic laminates, or thin melamine foil; veneered boards are sanded for polishing, and laminated boards are supplied ready-finished. Some plastic-laminate boards for countertops are made with finished profiled edges, while matching edging strips are available for melamine-faced and wood-veneer boards.

Oriented-strand board
This is a three-layer material made with long strands of softwood. The strands in each layer are laid in one direction, and each layer is perpendicular to the next in the same manner as plywood.

Flakeboard or waferboard
This type of board incorporates large shavings of wood which are laid horizontally and overlap one another. Flakeboard has greater tensile strength than standard particle board; although made for utilitarian applications, it can be used as a wallboard when finished with a clear varnish. It can also be stained.

WORKING MAN-MADE BOARDS

Although man-made boards are relatively easy to cut using woodworking hand tools and machines, the resin content in the boards can quickly dull cutting edges; tungsten-carbide-tipped (TCT) circular-saw blades and router cutters will keep their edge longer than standard steel ones.

The boards can be awkward to handle, due to their size, weight, or flexibility. Cutting a board into smaller sections requires clear space with adequate support, and possibly the help of another person.

Cutting by machine

Clean-cutting high-speed machine tools will give the best results when cutting man-made boards, but will dull quickly in the process. A universal saw blade with tungsten-carbide tipped teeth should be used for cutting a large amount of board. The board should be face-down when you use a hand-held power saw, and face-up for a table saw.

Cutting by hand

A 10 to 12PPI panel saw should be used for hand sawing; a tenon saw can be employed for smaller work. In either case, the saw should be held at a relatively shallow angle. To prevent breakout of the surface when severing fibers or laminate, all cutting lines should be scored with a sharp knife.

Threaded inserts

Supporting the board

The board should be supported close to the cut line and laid over the bench; sturdy boards can be supported on planks between trestles.

Large boards can be climbed upon, in order to reach the cutting line comfortably; a helper can support the offcut if it is unmanageable. The solo woodworker can saw between the planks or set up some means of supporting the offcut, to prevent it from breaking away before the cut is completed.

Planing the edge

Edges are planed in the same way as solid wood, but each edge is planed from both ends toward the middle, as with end grain, to prevent breakout of the core or surface veneers. The blade will need to be sharpened regularly during the course of planing.

Particleboard screws

Fixing boards

Screws in the edge of man-made boards are not as strong as those in the face. Pilot holes should be drilled in the edge of plywood to prevent splitting. The diameter of the screws should not exceed 25 percent of the board's thickness.

In particle board, screw-holding is dependent on the density of the board; most boards are relatively weak. Special particle board screws are better than standard ones. Pilot holes must always be drilled for both face or edge work and special fastenings or inserts can be used for improved holding (see page 93).

Blockboard and laminboard will hold screws well in the side edges, but not in the end grain.

MAKING
JOINTS

SQUARE-ENDED BUTT JOINT

It is possible to make flat frames and simple box structures utilizing square-cut corner joints. Use sawn wood for rough carpentry, but plane the wood square beforehand for good-quality cabinet work. Since glue alone is rarely adequate to make a sturdy butt joint, hold the parts together with fine nails or glued blocks of wood.

Box-frame joint

Flat-frame joint

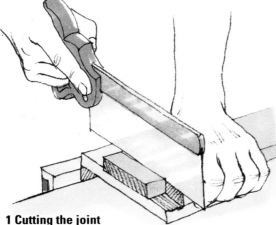

1 Cutting the joint
Mark out each piece of wood to length, using a knife and trysquare to mark the shoulders of the joint on all faces. Hold the work against a bench hook (see page 84), and saw down each shoulder, keeping to the waste side of the marked line.

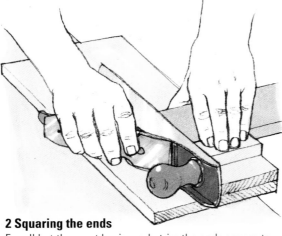

2 Squaring the ends
For all but the most basic work, trim the ends square to form a neat butt joint, using a bench plane and shooting board. Set the plane for a fine cut, and lubricate the running surfaces of the shooting board with a white candle or wax polish.

Reinforcing a butt joint
For additional strength, drive nails at an angle into the wood as shown. If you don't want the method of fixing to show on the outside of the joint, glue a corner block on the inside.

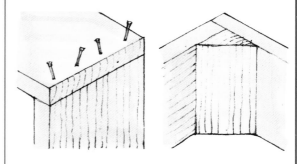

MAKING A SHOOTING BOARD
Cut a board 2ft (600mm) long from 1 x 9in (25x 225mm) close-grained hardwood. Make a second board the same length from similar 1 x 6in (25 x 150mm) wood. Glue the boards face to face to form a step.

To make a square-cutting version, glue and dowel a stop block at one end, at right angles to the stepped edge. For a miter shooting board, fix two stop blocks in the center at 45 degrees to the stepped edge.

Put a strip of wood on the underside for clamping the jig in a vise. Alternatively, leave the underside flat and clamp the jig between bench stops.

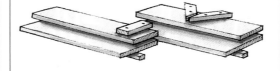

MITERED BUTT JOINT

The classic joint for picture frames, the mitered butt joint makes a neat right-angle corner without visible end grain. Cutting wood at 45 degrees produces a relatively large surface area of tangentially cut grain that glues well. For light-weight frames, just add glue and set the joint in a miter clamp.

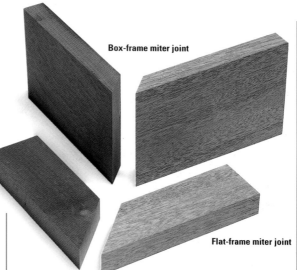

Box-frame miter joint

Flat-frame miter joint

Open joint caused by inaccurate cutting

Inside gap as a result of wood shrinking

Accurate miter cutting
Before you pick up a saw, always make sure the miter is exactly half the joint angle, or the joint will be gappy. In addition, use well-seasoned lumber or a gap may open up on the inside of the joint as the wood shrinks.

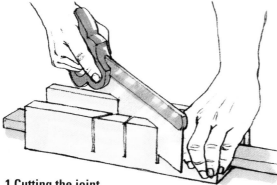

1 Cutting the joint
On each piece of wood, mark the sloping shoulder of the joint, using a knife and miter square. Extend the marked line across the adjacent faces with a trysquare. To remove the waste, either follow the marked lines by eye or use a miter box to guide the saw blade.

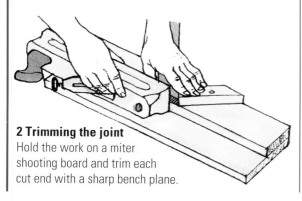

2 Trimming the joint
Hold the work on a miter shooting board and trim each cut end with a sharp bench plane.

Trimming a wide board
Since it is impossible to miter a wide piece of wood on a shooting board, clamp the work upright in a bench vise and trim the end grain with a finely set block plane. To prevent splitting, back up the work with a piece of scrap lumber.

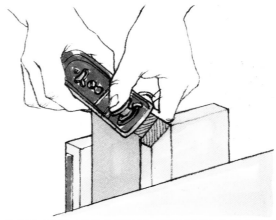

USING A MITER SAW
It pays to use a special jig called a miter saw to cut larger pieces of wood or moulded sections of framing. The workpiece can be held on edge or flat on the bed of the tool. The saw guide, which can be set to any angle, guarantees accurate joints.

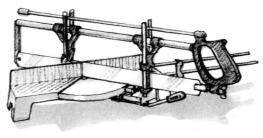

EDGE-TO-EDGE BUTT JOINT

Lumber selection is as important as good edge-to-edge joints when making a wide panel from solid wood. To make sure the panel will remain flat, try to use quarter-sawn wood—that is, with the end-grain growth rings running perpendicular to the face side of each board. If that is not possible, arrange them so the direction of ring growth alternates from one board to the next. Also try to make sure the surface grain on all boards runs in the same direction, to facilitate the final cleaning up of the panel with a plane. Before you get to work, number each board and mark the face side.

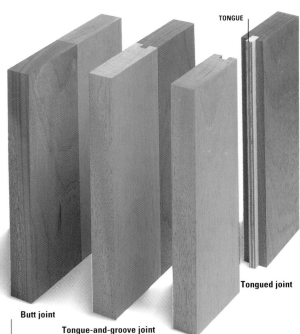

TONGUE

Butt joint

Tongue-and-groove joint

Tongued joint

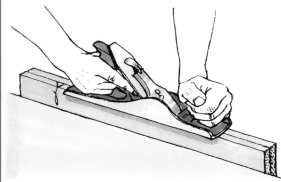

Planing edges square
With the face sides on the outside, set both boards back-to-back and level in a vise. Plane the edges straight and square, using the longest bench plane you can find, preferably a try plane.

Checking for straight edges
It is vital that the edges are straight if you intend to use a rubbed joint; check them using a metal straightedge. If the boards are to be clamped together, a very slight hollow is acceptable.

Matching edges
It is good practice to keep the edges as square as possible. However, provided boards have been planed as a pair, they will fit together and produce a flat surface, even when the edges are not exactly square.

CLAMPING JOINTS
Before adding glue, set prepared boards in bar clamps to check that the joints fit snugly. Use at least three clamps, alternated as shown, to counter any tendency for the panel to bow under pressure. Use scraps of softwood to protect the edges from bruising. When you have everything on hand, remove the clamps for gluing and reassembly of the joints.

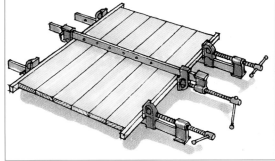

TONGUE-AND-GROOVE JOINT

Use a combination plane to cut a tongue-and-groove joint by hand. This kind of plane is similar to a standard plow plane, but comes with a wider range of cutters, including one designed to shape a tongue on the edge of a workpiece. Cut the tongue first, then change the cutter and plane a matching groove.

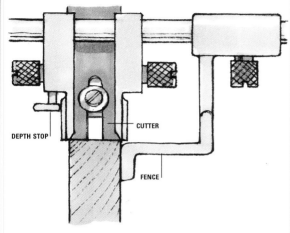

1 Adjusting the cutter
Clamp the work in a bench vise, face side toward you. Adjust the fence until the cutter is centered on the edge of the work. Provided the matching groove is also cut from the face side, it is not essential that the tongue is precisely on-center.

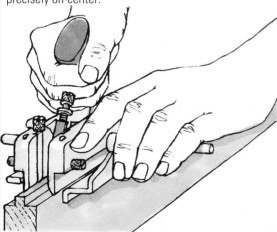

2 Cutting the tongue
Adjust the plane's depth stop to cut a tongue of the required size, then begin planing at the far end of the workpiece, gradually working backward as the tongue is formed.

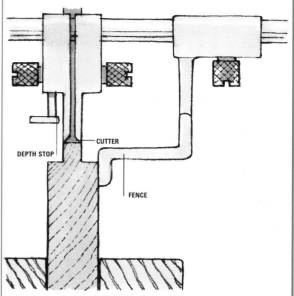

3 Cutting the groove
Select a plowing cutter that matches the width of the tongue, and fit it into the plane. Adjust the fence while sitting the cutter on top of the tongue; set the depth stop, making sure it will cut a groove slightly deeper than the tongue. Clamp the uncut board in the vise and cut the groove.

INCLUDING A TONGUE
A loose tongue has three advantages over using an integral one; it avoids decreasing the width of the boards; it gives the joint marginally greater strength; and a simple plow plane can be used to cut the grooves. Plane a groove down the center of each board and insert a separate tongue made from plywood or solid wood (ideally cross-grained). Glue one groove and tap the tongue into it, then brush glue into the other groove and assemble the joint in clamps as described opposite.

DOWELED FRAME JOINTS

Frames made with doweled butt joints are surprisingly strong. Nowadays, most factory-made furniture incorporates dowel joints, even for chair rails, which must be capable of resisting prolonged and considerable strain. In most cases, two dowels per joint are sufficient. Place them a minimum of ¼in (6mm) from both edges of the rail.

RAIL

LEG OR STILE

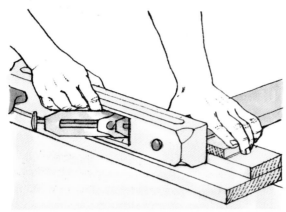

1 Cutting components to length
Saw each component to length and trim the ends of the rail square as described for making a square-ended butt joint (see page 68). Leave the stile or leg of a corner joint too long until the joint is finished.

2 Marking the joint
Clamp the two components in a vise with their joining surfaces flush. Using a trysquare, draw the center of each dowel hole across both components, then scribe a line centrally on each one with a marking gauge. Bore the dowel holes where the lines cross.

3 Boring dowel holes
Place the point of a dowel bit on the marked center and bore each hole in turn. Unless you are using a dowelling jig (see opposite) or a drill stand (see page 43), it pays to have someone standing to one side who can tell you when the drill bit is vertical.

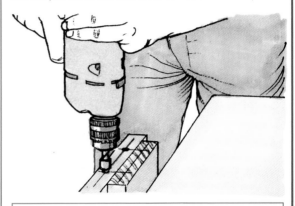

DOWELS
Ready-made dowels are manufactured from tough short-grain woods, such as ramin, birch, beech, or maple. They are chamfered at each end to make them easier to insert in the holes, and are fluted length-wise to allow excess glue to escape. Choose dowels that are about half the thickness of the workpieces; the length of each dowel should be approximately five times its diameter.

If you need a few dowels only, cut them from a length of dowel rod. Steady the rod on a bench hook and cut off short sections with a fine-tooth saw. Chamfer each dowel with a file, and saw a single glue slot.

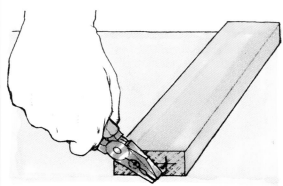

1 Using center points

For greater accuracy in marking out dowel joints, draw the center points on the end of the rail only, then drive in finishing nails where the lines cross. Cut off the nail heads with pliers, leaving short "spikes" projecting from the end grain.

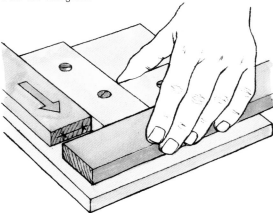

2 Marking the other component

Lay the leg or stile on its side and press the end of the rail against it, leaving two pinholes that mark the hole centers exactly. A simple right-angle jig keeps the components aligned.

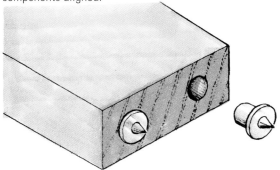

Ready-made center points

As an alternative to using finishing nails, bore dowel holes into the end of the rail, then slip into them purchased dowel points that will mark the side grain of the matching component.

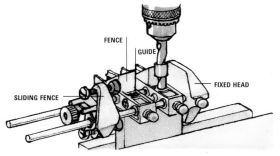

1 Doweling rails with a jig

Clamp the jig on the end of the rail, making sure the fixed head and side fences are located against the face side and edge of the workpiece. Drill both holes.

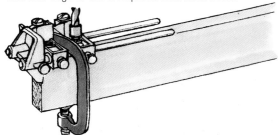

2 Doweling the stiles

Once you have drilled all the rails, remove the sliding fence and, without altering the other settings, turn the jig over and clamp it to the stile with a C-clamp. Bore dowel holes in the side grain.

DOWELING JIGS

It's worth acquiring a doweling jig for a project that requires a number of identical dowel joints. The jig not only guides the bit to bore perfectly vertical holes, it also dispenses with the need to mark out each and every joint separately. With one of the better jigs, you can mark out wide boards for cabinet work as well as rails and stiles. The type of jig shown here has a fixed head or fence from which measurements are taken, and a sliding fence that clamps the jig to the work-piece. Adjustable drill-bit guides and side fences position the dowel holes.

EDGE-TO-EDGE DOWEL JOINT

When constructing a wide solid-wood panel, you can make a particularly strong joint between boards by inserting a dowel every 9 to 12in (225 to 300mm).

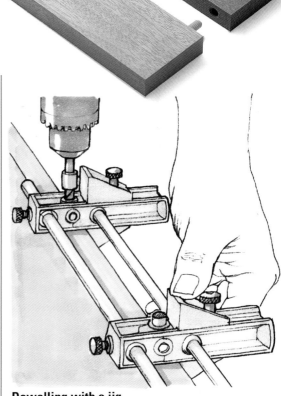

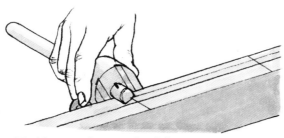

1 Marking an edge-to-edge joint
Clamp adjacent boards back-to-back in a vise and mark the dowel centers, using a trysquare and pencil. Scribe a line down the center of each board with a marking gauge.

2 Boring the holes
If possible, have a helper stand at one end of the workpiece, to tell you when the drill is upright as you bore each hole where the marked lines cross.

Dowelling with a jig
Remove both end fences of a doweling jig when boring holes in the edge of a wide board. Holding the side fences against the face side of the work, drill two holes. To drill subsequent holes, drop one drill-bit guide over a short dowel rod pushed into the last hole drilled.

USING A DEPTH STOP

Each hole should be slightly deeper than half the length of the dowel. To enable you to drill consistently deep holes, fit a plastic guide onto the drill bit (see right). Depth stops cost very little, but if you prefer, bind a strip of heavy tape around the drill bit to mark the appropriate level.

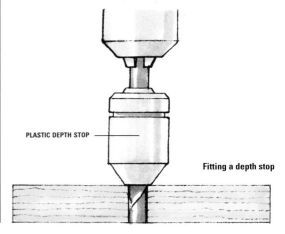

PLASTIC DEPTH STOP

Fitting a depth stop

CARCASS BUTT JOINTS

When constructing a carcass with butt joints that are reinforced with multiple dowels, it pays to buy extra-long slide rods and additional drill-bit guides for a doweling jig.

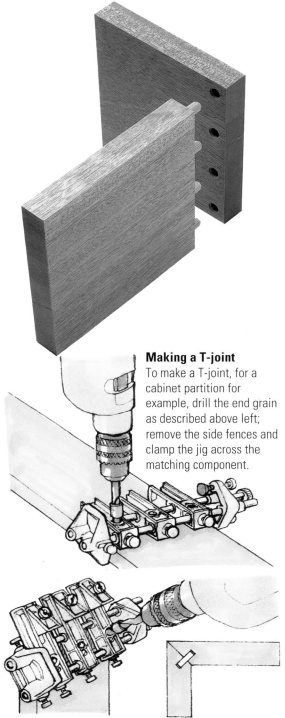

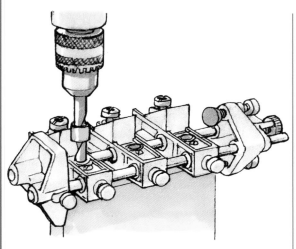

1 Doweling a corner joint

For a right-angle butt joint, drill the end grain first. Set the jig's side fences to position the dowel holes centrally on the thickness of the workpiece, and adjust the drill-bit guides to space the dowels 2 to 3in (50 to 75mm) apart. Make sure the fixed head is clamped against the face edge.

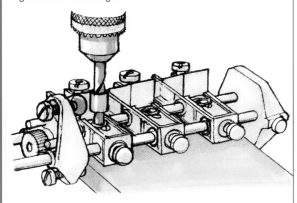

2 Drilling matching holes

Without changing any settings, invert the jig and clamp it to the inside of the other component, with the side fences butted against the end grain and the fixed head against the face edge. Attach a depth stop (see opposite) to the bit to make sure you don't drill right through the wood.

Making a T-joint

To make a T-joint, for a cabinet partition for example, drill the end grain as described above left; remove the side fences and clamp the jig across the matching component.

Doweling a mitered carcass joint

To make a dowel-reinforced miter joint, assemble a jig similar to that used for a right-angle butt joint (see left), and clamp it to the beveled end of the workpiece. Adjust the drill-bit guides to position the dowels toward the lower edge of the bevel. Having drilled the dowel holes, transfer the jig to the other mitered board and drill matching holes.

CORNER BRIDLE JOINT

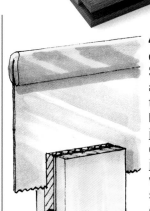

TENON MEMBER

MORTISE MEMBER

A corner bridle joint is adequate for relatively lightweight frames, provided they are not subjected to sideways pressure, which tends to force bridle joints out of square. The strength of the bridle is improved considerably if you insert two dowels through the side of the joint after the glue has set.

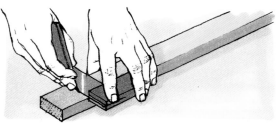

1 Marking out the shoulders
Taking each tenon member in turn, mark square shoulders all around, allowing for a tenon that is slightly too long so it can be planed flush after the joint is complete. Use a marking knife, but apply light pressure across both edges. Mark out the mortise member similarly, but this time use a pencil.

2 Scribing the tenon
Set the points of a mortise gauge to one-third the thickness of the wood, and adjust the tool's stock (fence) to center the points on the edge of the work. Scribe the width of the tenon on both edges and across the end.

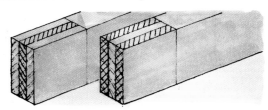

3 Marking out the open mortise
Use the same gauge to mark the sides of the open mortise, then use a marking knife to score the short shoulders at the base of the mortise, between the gauged lines. Mark the waste wood with a pencil on both components so that you don't get confused when cutting the joint.

4 Cutting the open mortise
Select a drill bit that approximates the width of the mortise, and bore a hole into the waste wood just above the shoulder line on opposite sides of the joint. Set the wood in a vise and saw on the waste side of both gauged lines, down to the hole at the base of the mortise. Chisel the shoulder square.

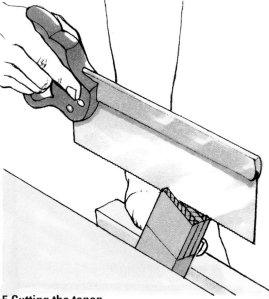

5 Cutting the tenon
With the work clamped in a vise, saw both sides of the tenon down to the shoulder (see mortise and tenon, page 89). Lay the workpiece on its side on a bench hook and saw each shoulder line to remove the waste wood.

MITERED BRIDLE JOINT

The mitered bridle is cut in a similar way to the conventional corner joint, but is a more attractive alternative for framing, because end grain appears on one edge only.

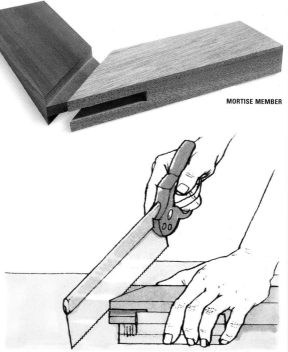

TENON MEMBER

MORTISE MEMBER

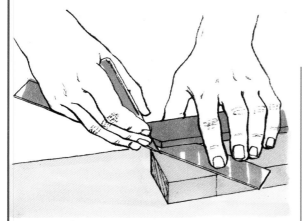

1 Marking the joint
Cut the components exactly to length. Mark the width of the parts on each end and square the shoulders all around, using a trysquare and pencil. Mark the sloping face of the miter on both sides of each component with a knife and miter square.

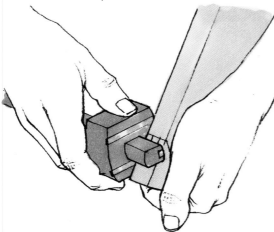

2 Gauging the tenon and open mortise
Set the pins of a mortise gauge to one-third the thickness of the wood, and adjust the stock to centralize the pair of pins on the edge of the work. Scribe the width of the tenon on the inside edge and across the end grain of the appropriate member. On the mortise member, scribe similar lines across the end and on both edges.

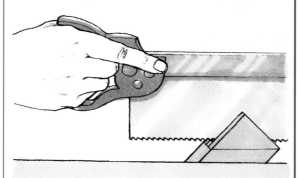

3 Cutting the open mortise
Cut out the waste from the mortise as described for a conventional corner bridle joint (see opposite), then hold the work on a bench hook and saw down the marked line to miter both cheeks of the joint. If the miters are not perfect, shave them with a block plane.

4 Cutting the tenon
Clamp the tenon member at an angle in a vise and saw down to the mitered shoulder on both sides of the tenon; keep the saw blade just to the waste side of the line. Holding the work on a bench hook, saw along both mitered shoulders to remove the waste. If necessary, trim the mitered surfaces with a shoulder plane.

T-BRIDLE JOINT

The T-bridle serves as an intermediate support for a frame and, with modifications, is sometimes used to join a table leg to the underframe when a long rail requires support. Unlike the corner bridle, which is relatively weak under sideways pressure, the T-bridle is similar in strength to the mortise-and-tenon joint.

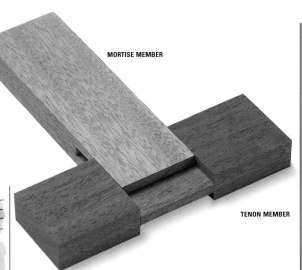

MORTISE MEMBER

TENON MEMBER

1 Marking the shoulders
Mark the width of the mortise member on the tenon member, using a marking knife to score square shoulders all around. Apply light pressure only across the edges. Allowing for slightly overlong cheeks on the mortise member, mark square shoulders all around with a pencil and trysquare.

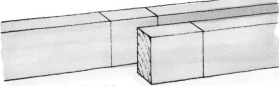

2 Gauging the joint
Set the pins of a mortise gauge to one-third the thickness of the wood, and adjust the stock to center the pair of pins on the edge of the workpiece. Scribe parallel lines between the marked shoulders on the tenon member, then mark similar lines on the end and both edges of the mortise member.

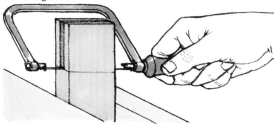

3 Cutting the open mortise
Cut the mortise as described for a corner bridle joint (see page 76). Alternatively, saw down both sides of the open mortise with a tenon saw, then use a coping saw to remove the waste, cutting as close to the shoulder as possible. If necessary, trim the shoulder square with a sharp chisel.

4 Cutting the tenon member
On both sides of the tenon member, saw the shoulders down to the gauged lines, then make three or four similar saw cuts in between. With the work held firmly, chop out the waste with a mallet and chisel, working from each edge toward the middle. Having assembled the joint, allow the glue to set, then plane the ends of the mortise cheeks flush with the tenon member.

TABLE-LEG VERSION
When joining a square leg to a table underframe, make the "tenon" about two-thirds the thickness of the rail. Offset the open mortise so that a slightly over-hanging table top can conceal the leg's end grain.

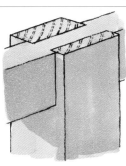

LAP JOINT

A basic lap joint is only marginally stronger than a straightforward butt joint, but it is an improvement in appearance, since most of the end grain is concealed. As a result, it is sometimes used as a relatively simple way of connecting a drawer front to drawer sides.

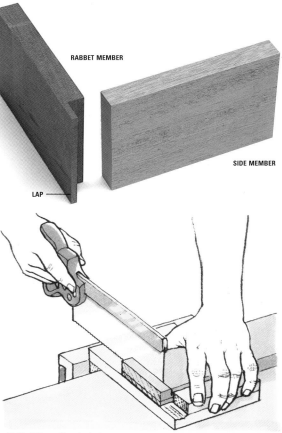

RABBET MEMBER

SIDE MEMBER

LAP

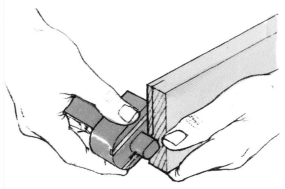

1 Marking out the rabbet
Cut and plane both members square. Adjust a marking gauge to about one-quarter of the thickness of the rabbet member, and scribe a line across the end grain, working from the face side. Continue the line on both edges, down to the level of the shoulder.

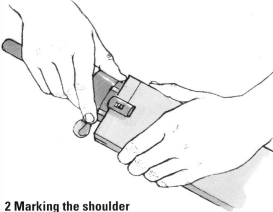

2 Marking the shoulder
Set a cutting gauge to match the thickness of the side member, and scribe a shoulder line parallel to the end grain on the back of the rabbet member. Continue the shoulder line across both edges to meet the lines already scribed.

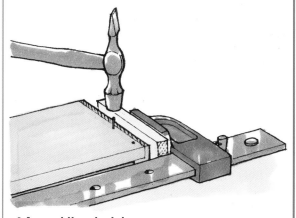

3 Cutting the joint
Clamp the rabbet member upright in a vise. Following the line scribed across the end grain, saw down to the shoulder line. Lay the work face down on a bench hook and cut down the shoulder line with a tenon saw to remove the waste. Make a neat joint by cleaning up the rabbet with a shoulder plane.

4 Assembling the joint
Glue and clamp the joint, then drive panel pins or small finishing nails through the side member. Sink the nails with a nail punch and fill the holes.

THROUGH DADO JOINT

This simple through joint shows on the front edges of side panels. It is suitable for rough shelving, or for cupboards with lay-on doors that cover the front edges. If you plan to lip the boards, it is best to apply the lippings first, so it is easier to plane them flush.

SIDE PANEL

SHELF

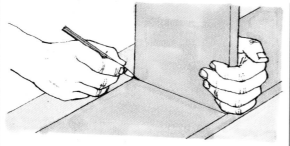

1 Marking the face of the side panel
Measure the width of the dado from the shelf, then score the two lines across the workpiece, using a trysquare and marking knife.

2 Marking the edges
Square the same lines onto the edges of the panel, then scribe a line between them, using a marking gauge set to about ¼in (6mm).

3 Sawing the dado shoulders
To make it easier to locate a saw across a wide panel, take a chisel and pare a shallow V-shape groove up to the marked line on both sides of the housing, then use a tenon saw to cut each shoulder down to the lines scribed on each edge.

4 Removing the waste
Pare out the waste from a narrow panel with a chisel, working from each side toward the middle.

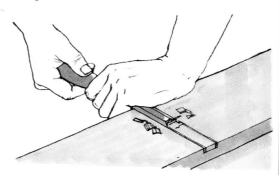

USING A ROUTER PLANE
Having chiseled out most of the waste, pare the bottom of a dado level, using a special router plane fitted with a narrow, adjustable L-shape blade. When a panel is too wide to use a chisel conveniently, remove all the waste in stages by making several passes with the router plane, lowering the cutter each time the dado is level.

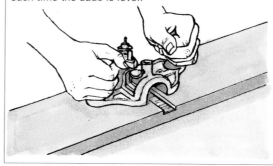

DOVETAIL DADO JOINT

When cutting this joint by hand, incorporate a single dovetail along one side of the dado. Double-sided dovetails are best cut with a power router. Since the shelf member must be slid into place from one end of the housing, the joint needs to be cut accurately.

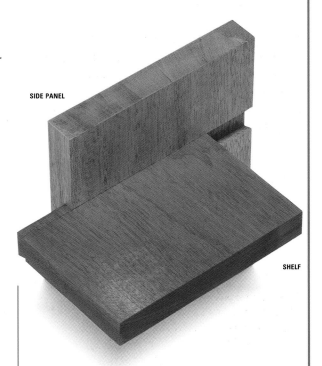

SIDE PANEL

SHELF

1 Marking the shoulder
Set a cutting gauge to about one-third the thickness of the wood and score a shoulder line on the underside of the shelf. Using a trysquare and pencil, continue the line across both edges.

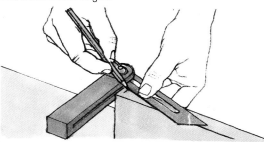

2 Marking the dovetail angle
Set a sliding bevel to a dovetail angle (see page 90), and mark the slope of the joint, running from the bottom corner to the marks drawn on both edges.

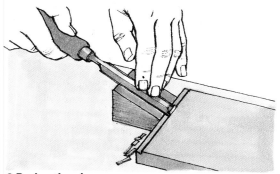

3 Paring the slope
Saw along the shoulder line, down to the base of the slope, then pare out the waste with a chisel. To help keep the angle constant, use a shaped block of wood to guide the blade.

4 Cutting the dado
Mark out the dado as described opposite, and use the sliding bevel to mark the dovetail on both edges of the panel. Saw both shoulders, using a beveled block of wood to guide the saw blade when cutting the dovetail. Remove the waste with a router plane, or use a bevel-edge chisel to clear the undercut.

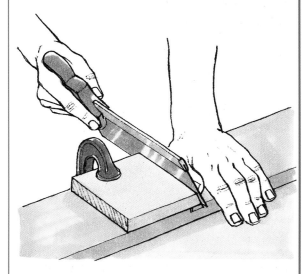

STOPPED DADO JOINT

For decorative effect, the housing is often stopped short of the front edge of the side panel by about ⅜ to ½in (9 to 12mm). Occasionally, the shelf is also cut short, fitting the housing exactly—useful when making a cabinet with inset doors. Generally, however, the front edge of the shelf is notched so its front edge finishes flush with the side panel. The instructions below explain how to cut the joint with handtools, but you could use a power router to cut a stopped dado.

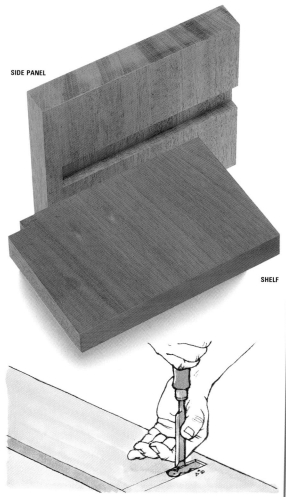

SIDE PANEL

SHELF

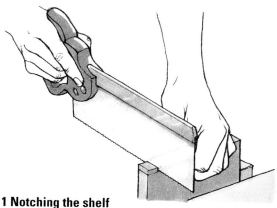

1 Notching the shelf
Set a marking gauge to the planned depth of the dado, and use it to mark the notch on the front corner of the shelf. Cut the notch with a tenon saw.

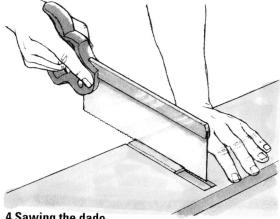

3 Cutting the stopped end
To provide clearance for sawing the dado, first drill out the waste at the stopped end and trim the shoulders square with a chisel.

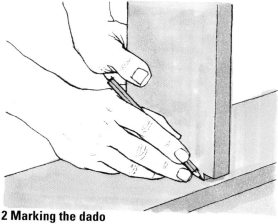

2 Marking the dado
Use the notched shelf to mark the dimensions of the dado, then score the lines across the side panel with a trysquare and marking knife. Scribe the stopped end of the dado with a marking gauge.

4 Sawing the dado
Saw along the scored shoulders down to the base of the dado, then pare out the waste from the back edge with a chisel, or use a router plane.

DADO AND RABBET JOINT

The dado and rabbet joint is a variation on the basic lap joint, adapted for making box-frame or cabinet corners. The dado should be no deeper than about one-quarter the thickness of the wood, and about the same in width.

SIDE PANEL

HORIZONTAL MEMBER

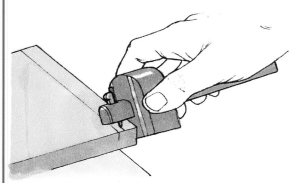

1 Marking the dado
Cut and plane square the ends of both components. Set a cutting gauge to the thickness of the horizontal member, and lightly scribe the bottom edge of the dado across the side panel and down both edges. Reset the gauge and scribe the top edge of the dado in the same way.

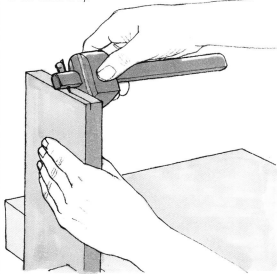

2 Marking the tongue
Using the gauge with the same setting, mark the tongue on the end and down both edges of the horizontal member, working from the face side.

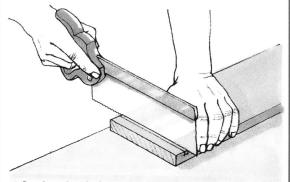

3 Marking the rabbet shoulder
Reset the gauge to about one-third the thickness of the side panel, and mark the rabbet shoulder line across the face side and down both edges of the horizontal member. Form the rabbet by removing the waste with a saw and cleaning up with a shoulder plane.

4 Cutting the dado
Mark the depth of the dado on the edges of the side panel and remove the waste with a saw and chisel, as described for a through dado joint (see page 80).

83

CROSS LAP JOINT

With a cross lap joint, both halves of the joint are identical. Although the joint is equally strong whichever way the components run, convention dictates that the vertical member or divider appears to run through, although, in reality, half the thickness is removed from each piece of wood.

RAIL

DIVIDER

1 Marking the shoulders
Lay both components side by side and score the shoulder lines across them, using a trysquare and marking knife. Continue both sets of marked lines half-way down each edge.

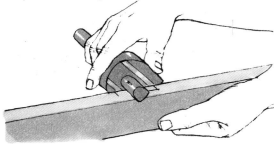

2 Marking the depth of the joint
Set a marking gauge to exactly half the thickness of the wood, and scribe a line between the shoulders marked on the edges of both components.

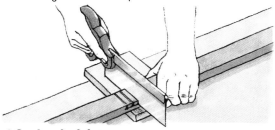

3 Cutting the joint
Saw halfway through both pieces of wood on the waste side of each shoulder line. Divide the waste wood between the shoulders with one or two additional saw cuts.

4 Chopping out the waste
Clamp the work in a vice and chisel out the waste, working from each side towards the middle of each component. Pare the bottom of each resulting recess flat with a chisel.

MAKING A BENCH HOOK
Cut a baseboard about 210 x 8in (50 x 200mm) from close-grained hardwood such as beech or maple, ¾in (18mm) thick. Cut two stop blocks 6in (50mm) long and 1½in (38mm) wide. Glue and dowel the blocks flush with the ends of the baseboard, on opposite faces. Inset the blocks by 1in (25mm) from each long edge; this means the guide can be used by left- or right-handed woodworkers.

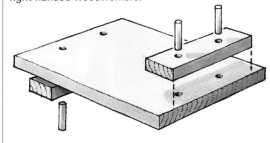

END LAP JOINT

You can construct a simple framework, using a lap joint at each corner. However, since this type of joint relies almost entirely on glue for strength, you may need to reinforce it with wood screws or hardwood dowels. The mitered lap joint is a refined version, but it has even less gluing area.

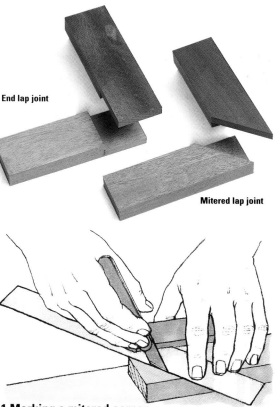

End lap joint

Mitered lap joint

1 Marking the basic lap joint
Lay the components side by side, and mark the shoulder line across both of them. Continue the lines down each edge.

2 Gauging the depth
Set a marking gauge to half the thickness of the wood and scribe a line up both edges and across the end grain. Remove the waste with a tenon saw, cutting downward from the end grain, followed by sawing across the shoulder.

1 Marking a mitered corner
Mark and cut one component as described left, then cut the lap to 45 degrees. Score the angled shoulder line across the face of the second component, using a knife and miter square, then scribe the center line up the inner edge and across the end grain.

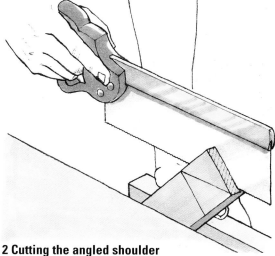

2 Cutting the angled shoulder
Clamp the work at an angle in a vise and saw on the waste side of the center line, down to the shoulder. Lay the work on a bench hook, and remove the waste by sawing down the shoulder line.

MID LAP JOINT

A means of joining an intermediate support to a frame, the mid-lap joint is a combination of the cross lap and end lap versions.

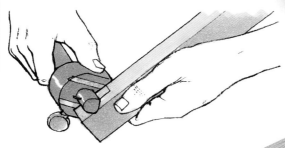

1 Marking out the joint
Taking the dimensions from the relevant components, score the shoulder lines with a knife and trysquare, and scribe the depth of the joint on each workpiece with a marking gauge.

2 Cutting the recess
Chisel out the waste from between the shoulders. Use the long edge of the chisel blade to check that the bottom of the recess is flat.

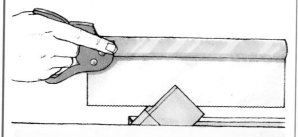

3 Sawing the lap
Saw down to the shoulder, keeping the saw blade just to the waste side of the gauged line. You may find it easier to keep the cut vertical if you tilt the work away from you while sawing down one edge. Turn the work around and saw down the other edge, then finish off by sawing squarely down to the shoulder.

4 Removing the waste
With the wood resting on a bench hook, saw down the shoulder line to remove the waste. If necessary, trim the shoulder square with a chisel or shoulder plane (see page 31).

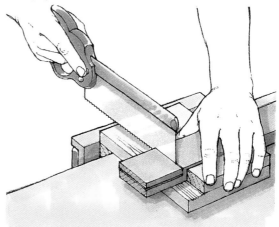

DOVETAILED LAP JOINT

Incorporate a dovetail to increase the strength of a T-halving joint. It is only marginally more difficult to make than the standard square-shoulder joint.

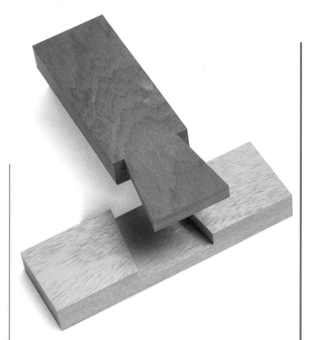

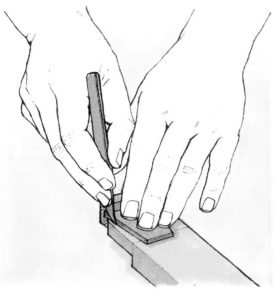

1 Marking the lap dovetail
Having marked out and cut a lap in the conventional manner (see opposite), use a template and knife to mark the dovetail on the workpiece.

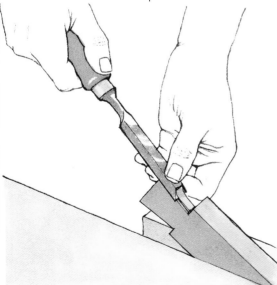

2 Shaping the lap dovetail
Saw the short shoulders on both sides of the lap, then pare away the waste with a chisel to form the sloping sides of the dovetail.

3 Marking and cutting the recess
Using the dovetailed lap as a template, score the shoulders of the recess on the cross member. Mark the depth of the recess with a marking gauge (see page 18), and then remove the waste wood with a tenon saw and chisel.

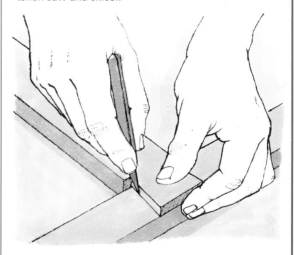

MAKING A TEMPLATE
Cut a tapered plywood tongue, with one side angled for marking dovetails in softwood and the other for dovetailing hardwoods (see page 90). Glue the tongue into a slot cut in a hardwood stock.

THROUGH MORTISE AND TENON

The through joint, where the tenon passes right through the leg, is used a great deal for constructional frames of all kinds. With the end grain showing, possibly with wooden wedges used to spread the tenon, it is an attractive, businesslike joint. Always cut the mortise first, since it is easier to make the tenon fit exactly than the other way around.

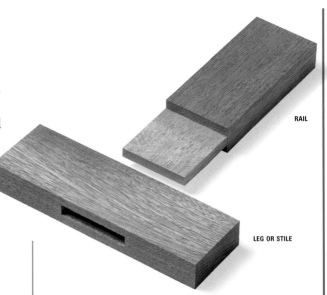

RAIL

LEG OR STILE

1 Marking the length of the mortise
Mark the position and length of the mortise, using the rail as a template. Square the lines all around with a pencil.

2 Scribing the mortise
Set a mortise gauge to match the width of the mortise chisel to be used, and then scribe the mortise centrally between the squared lines on both of its edges.

3 Marking the tenon shoulders
Mark the shoulders on the rail, allowing for slightly overlong tenons that can be planed flush when the joint is complete. Score the shoulder lines with a marking knife.

4 Scribing the tenon
Without adjusting the settings, use the mortise gauge to scribe the tenon on both edges and across the end of the rail.

PROPORTIONS OF A MORTISE AND TENON

Cut the tenon for a standard joint to approximately one-third the thickness of the rail, the exact size being determined by the chisel used to cut the mortise. Tenon thickness can be increased when the leg or mortise member is thicker than the rail.

A tenon normally runs the full width of the rail, but should the rail be unusually wide, it is best to incorporate a pair of tenons, one above the other, to avoid weakening the leg with an excessively long mortise. This type of joint is known as a double mortise and tenon. Twin tenons, cut side by side, are required when a rail is set horizontally.

Make the depth of a stopped mortise about three-quarters the width of the leg or stile.

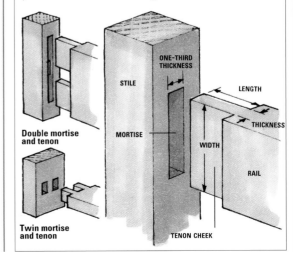

ONE-THIRD THICKNESS

STILE

LENGTH

Double mortise and tenon

MORTISE

THICKNESS

WIDTH

RAIL

Twin mortise and tenon

TENON CHEEK

5 Chopping the mortise

Clamp the work to a bench so that you can stand at one end of the stile. Holding the chisel vertically, drive it ⅛ to ¼in (3 to 6mm) into the wood at the center of the marked mortise. Work backward in short stages, making similar cuts and making sure you stop about 1⁄16in (2mm) from the end of the mortise.

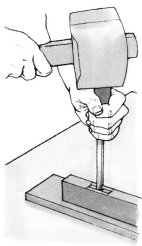

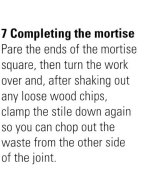

6 Removing the waste

Turn the mortise chisel around and chop the wood in stages toward the other end of the mortise. Lever out the waste with the chisel, then chop out another section of wood until you have cut halfway through the stile.

7 Completing the mortise

Pare the ends of the mortise square, then turn the work over and, after shaking out any loose wood chips, clamp the stile down again so you can chop out the waste from the other side of the joint.

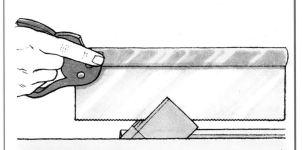

8 Sawing the tenon

Clamp the rail in a vise, set at an angle so the end grain faces away from you. Saw down to the shoulder on the waste side of each scribed line. Turn the work around and saw down to the shoulder line on the other side of the tenon.

9 Cutting square

Clamp the work upright and saw parallel to the shoulder on both sides of the tenon, taking care not to overrun the marks.

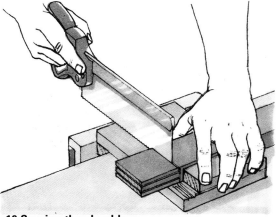

10 Sawing the shoulders

Holding the rail on a bench hook, remove the waste by sawing down the shoulder line on each side of the tenon. If necessary, pare the sides of the tenon with a chisel until it fits the mortise snugly.

THROUGH DOVETAIL JOINT

The ability to cut tight-fitting dovetail joints seems to be regarded as the ultimate test of the woodworker's skill. It is also, undeniably, one of the most efficient joints for constructing boxes and cabinets from solid wood. Through dovetails, the most basic form of the joint, are visible on both sides of a corner.

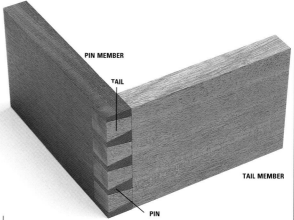

PIN MEMBER

TAIL

TAIL MEMBER

PIN

1 Scribing the shoulder line
Plane square the ends of both workpieces and, with a cutting gauge set to the thickness of the pin member, scribe the shoulder line for the tails on all sides of the other workpiece.

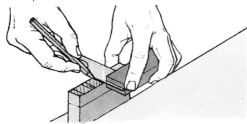

2 Spacing the tails
A good hand-cut joint has equal-sized tails matched with relatively narrow pins. Pencil a line across the end grain, ¼in (6mm) from each edge of the work, then divide the distance between the lines equally, depending on the required number of tails. Measure ⅛in (3mm) on each side of these marks and square pencil lines across the end.

3 Marking out the tails
Mark the sloping sides of each tail on the face side of the workpiece, using an adjustable bevel or a ready-made dovetail template. Mark the waste with a pencil.

4 Cutting the tails
Clamp the work at an angle in a vise so you can saw vertically beside each dovetail. When you have reached the last tail in the row, cant the work in the other direction and saw down the other side of each tail.

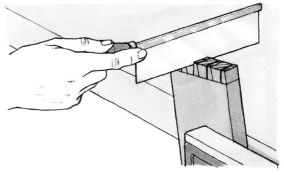

DOVETAIL ANGLES
The sides of a dovetail must slope at the optimum angle. An exaggerated slope results in weak short grain at the tips of the dovetail, while insufficient taper invariably leads to a slack joint. Ideally, mark a 1:8 angle for hardwoods, but increase the angle to 1:6 for softwoods. The proportion of each tail is a matter of personal interpretation, but a row of small, regularly spaced tails looks better than a few large ones, and also makes a stronger joint.

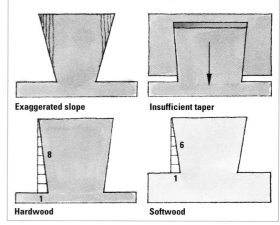

Exaggerated slope   **Insufficient taper**

8

6

1   1

Hardwood   **Softwood**

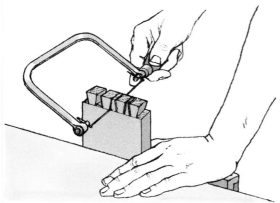

5 Removing the waste

Set the work horizontally in the vise so you can remove the corner waste with the dovetail saw, then cut the waste from between the tails, this time using a coping saw.

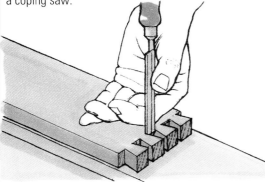

6 Trimming the shoulders

Use a bevel-edge chisel to trim what remains of the waste from between the tails. Finish flush with the shoulder line.

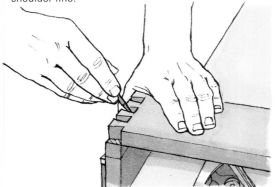

7 Marking the pins

Set the cutting gauge to the thickness of the tail member and scribe shoulder lines for the pins on the other component. Coat its end grain with chalk and clamp it upright in a vise. Position the cut tails precisely on the end of the workpiece, then mark their shape in the chalk with a pointed scriber or knife.

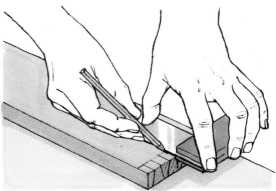

8 Marking cutting lines

Align a trysquare with the marks scored in the chalk, and draw parallel lines down to the shoulder on both sides of the work. Hatch the waste between the pins with a pencil.

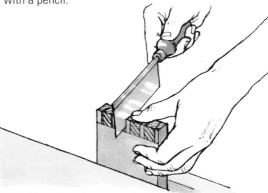

9 Cutting the pins

Make fine saw cuts on both sides of each pin, following the angled lines marked across the chalked end grain. Finish flush with the shoulder.

10 Trimming the joint

Remove most of the waste wood with a coping saw, and pare the shoulders with a chisel. Assemble the joint dry, trimming any tight spots until the joint fits cleanly and snugly.

BOLT AND BARREL NUT

This is a strong and positive fixing for all types of frame construction where the end of a rail meets the side of a leg or other vertical member. The bolt passes through a counterbored hole in the leg and into the end of the rail, where it is then screwed into a threaded barrel nut located in a stopped hole. A screw slot in the end of the nut allows you to align the threaded hole with the bolt. A wooden locating dowel fitted in the end of the rail makes assembly easier and prevents the rail from turning as the bolt is tightened.

3 Fitting the locating dowel
Tap a panel pin into the end of the rail on its center line, about ½in (12mm) from one edge. Crop the head off the pin, then assemble and tighten the fitting. Dismantle the joint, and drill a ¼in (6mm) stopped hole in the leg where the cropped pin left a mark. Remove the pin and drill the rail in the same way as the leg, then glue a short dowel in the hole.

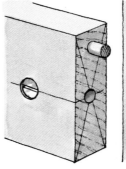

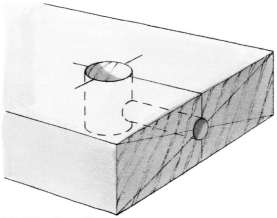

1 Drilling the rail
Draw diagonals across the end of the rail to find the center, and bore a clearance hole for the bolt where the lines cross. Calculate the distance from the end of the rail for the barrel nut, and drill a stopped hole in the side of the rail to intercept the bolt hole.

T-NUTS AND BOLTS
A T-nut is an internally threaded collar with an integral spiked washer that provides a firm anchor for a bolt fixing. A relatively crude fixing, it is probably best reserved for upholstered frames.

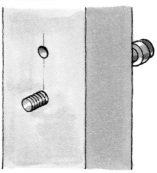

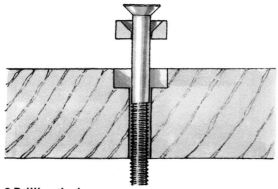

2 Drilling the leg
Mark and drill a counterbored clearance hole for the bolt and collar in the leg.

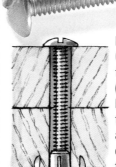

Fitting a T-nut
Clamp the components together and drill a ⁵⁄₁₆in (8mm) clearance hole through both parts. Tap the nut into the back of one component and pass the bolt through the other. Tighten the bolt to pull the parts together, and seat the nut securely in the wood.

SCREW SOCKETS

BLOCK JOINTS

Threaded-metal screw sockets provide secure fixing points for bolting together wood frames or man-made boards. A coarse thread on the outside of each fixture pulls the socket into a stopped hole drilled in the face of one component. A finer thread on the inside of the fixture receives a metal bolt that holds the other component in place.

This inexpensive, surface-mounted fixture consists of interlocking plastic blocks screwed on the inside of cabinet corners. Molded dowels on one half of the joint locate with sockets in the other. When two panels have been joined at right angles, the block fixtures are clamped together with a bolt.

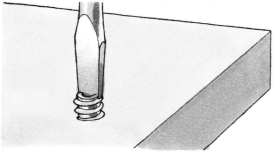

1 Fitting a socket
Bore a 5⁄16in (8mm) diameter stopped hole deep enough to set the socket just below the surface of the workpiece. Drive the fixture into the hole, using a screwdriver in the slot cut across the end of the socket.

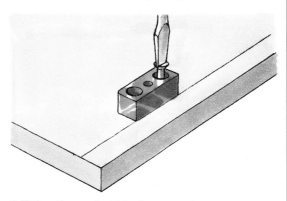

1 Fitting the socket blocks
Mark the thickness of the board on the inside of the carcass side panel. Mark the positions of two block joints about 2in (50mm) from the front and back edges. Align the base of each socket block with the marked lines, and screw it to the panel.

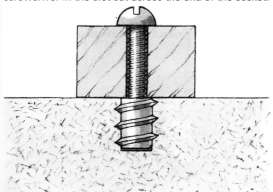

2 Assembling the components
Mark the center of a clearance hole for the bolt in the other component and drill right through it, taking care not to splinter the wood fibers on the underside. Assemble the two halves of the joint, clamping them tightly with the bolt.

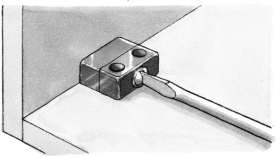

2 Fitting the dowel blocks
Holding the panels together at right angles, fit the mating dowel blocks and mark their fixing holes on the other board. Screw the blocks in place, and assemble the joint with the clamping bolts.

CLAMPING JOINTS

When gluing up any assembly, it pays to prepare the work area and rehearse the procedure in advance. This avoids delays that could lead to complications, especially when you are using a fast-setting adhesive. Assemble the parts without glue to work out how many clamps you need and to allow you to adjust them to fit the work. You will find a helper useful when clamping large or complicated assemblies.

It isn't necessary to glue every joint at once. For example, glue the legs and end rails of a table frame first; when these are set, glue the side rails between them. (Also see page 70 for clamping.)

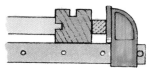

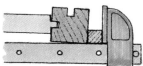
Block aligned

Block misaligned

CLAMPING A FRAME

The majority of frame and carcass joints need clamping in order to hold the assembly square until the adhesive sets. Prepare a pair of bar or pipe cramps, adjusting them so the assembled frame fits between the jaws, allowing for softwood blocks to protect the work from the metal clamp heads. Carefully position the blocks to align with each joint—a misplaced or undersized block can distort the joint and bruise the wood.

MAKING RUBBED JOINTS

Small, accurately cut edge-to-edge joints can be assembled without clamps. Apply glue to both parts and rub them together, squeezing out air and adhesive until atmospheric pressure holds the surfaces in contact while the glue sets.

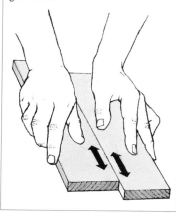

1 Aligning the clamps

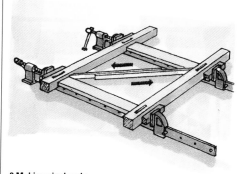
2 Making pinch rods

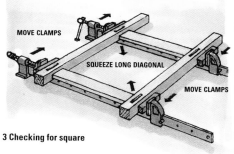
MOVE CLAMPS
SQUEEZE LONG DIAGONAL
MOVE CLAMPS
3 Checking for square

1 Aligning the clamps
Apply adhesive evenly to both parts of each joint. Assemble the frame, making sure that the clamps are perfectly aligned with their respective rails, and gradually tighten the jaws to close the joints. Wipe off excess adhesive squeezed from the joints using a damp cloth.

2 Making pinch rods
You can check the accuracy of a small frame with a trysquare at each corner, but for larger ones, measure the diagonals to make sure they are identical. Make a pair of pinch rods from thin strips of wood, planing a bevel on one end of each rod. Holding the rods back to back, slide them sideways until they fit diagonally across the frame, with a beveled end tucked into each corner.

3 Checking for square
Holding the pinch rods together firmly, lift them out of the frame and check to see if they fit the other diagonal exactly. If the diagonals are different, slacken the clamps and set them at a slight angle to pull the frame square, then check the diagonals again.

FINISHING
WOOD

FILLING CRACKS AND HOLES

STOPPER

WAX FILLER STICKS

ELECTRIC
SOLDERING IRON

SHELLAC STICKS

Although any woodworker rejects lumber with glaring defects such as end splits and shakes, it is difficult to guarantee that a batch of wood will be completely faultless, without at least some minor cracks or evidence of wood-boring insects. Try as you may to select only the better sections of the wood, you must invariably fill or patch a few cracks and holes before starting to sand to a smooth finish. However, there are a number of materials and techniques you can draw upon, depending on the dimensions of the crack or hole, and the type of finish you intend to apply.

Cellulose filler for paintwork
You can use a commercially prepared or homemade stopper when preparing wood for painting, or you can fill small holes and cracks with ordinary decorator's cellulose filler. Supplied ready-made in tubs or as a dry powder for mixing with water, cellulose filler is applied and sanded flush like wood putty.

Wood putty or stopper
Traditional filler made from wood dust mixed with glue still has its uses, but most wood finishers prefer to employ commercially prepared wood putty, or stopper, sold as a thick paste in tubes or small cans, for filling indentations. Stoppers are made in a range of colors to resemble common wood species.

Most stoppers are one-part pastes, formulated for either interior or exterior woodwork. Once set, they can be planed, sanded, and drilled along with the surrounding wood; they remain slightly flexible, to absorb any subsequent movement that may be caused by the wood shrinking and expanding.

Catalyzed two-part stoppers, intended primarily for larger repairs, set even harder than the standard pastes. Take care not to overfill when using them, or you may find yourself using up a great deal of sandpaper just to achieve a flush surface. Use a two-part filler if you want to build up an edge or broken corner.

Reconstituting stopper
To keep wood stopper in usable condition, replace the lid or screw cap as soon as you have taken enough for your requirements. If you find that stored water-based stopper has stiffened, try standing the can in warm water or place the container on a radiator to make the filler pliable.

MAKING YOUR OWN STOPPER
To make your own filler, collect sawdust or, better still, the dust created by sanding a workpiece or a wood scrap. Mix plenty of dust with a little PVA glue to make a thick paste—a glue-rich filler tends to reject stains and polishes, creating a visible repair. As an alternative to glue, try using some of the finish you intend to apply. If color-matching proves to be a problem, try adding a drop or two of compatible stain or some powdered pigment to the mix.

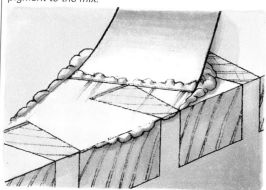

Disguising joints
Filled shoulder lines are almost always discernible, but you can make passable repairs to gappy joints that have visible end grain using a homemade filler.

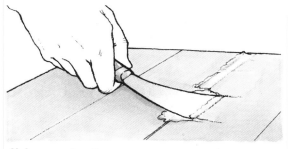

Using wood putty
Make sure the wood is clean and dry. Using a flexible filling knife, press putty into the indentations, leaving the filler slightly raised for sanding flush after it has set. Drag the knife across a crack to fill it, then smooth the putty by running the blade lengthwise. Fill deep holes in stages, leaving the stopper to harden between applications.

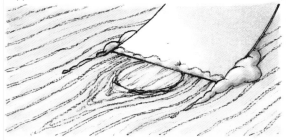

Filling large holes
Plug deep knotholes with solid wood. When the glue has set, fill gaps around the patch with wood stopper.

Coloring filler to match
To match the color of your workpiece, make a test piece by applying stain and one finish coat to a scrap of the same wood. Select a filler that resembles the lightest background color of the wood and, using a white ceramic tile as a palette, add compatible wood dye one drop at a time. Blend the dye into the filler with a filling knife to achieve the required tone. Mix a color that is slightly darker than your test piece to allow for the fact that putty will be a shade lighter when it dries.

Alternatively, add powdered pigments to color the filler, plus a drop of compatible solvent if the paste becomes too stiff.

FILLER STICKS
Sticks of solidified shellac in various colors are made for melting into holes in the wood or for building up broken moldings. Shellac can be used as a preparatory stopper for use with most surface finishes However, it may prevent an acid-catalyzed cold-cure lacquer from curing properly.

Carnauba wax, mixed with pigments and resins, is ideal for plugging small wormholes. Although wax filler can be applied to bare wood that is to be French-polished or waxed, it is often best to wait until the wood is finished.

Wax sticks are made in a range of colors. If necessary, cut pieces of wax from different sticks, blending them with the tip of a soldering iron to match a specific color. This method of filling is known as beaumontage.

Filling with shellac
Use a heated knife blade or a soldering iron to melt the tip of a shellac stick, allowing it to drip into the hole. While it is still soft, press the shellac flat with a wood chisel dipped in water. As soon as the filler hardens, pare it flush with a sharp chisel, finishing with a fine abrasive.

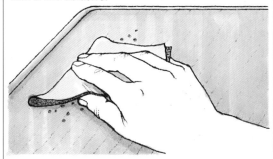

Using wax filling sticks
Cut off a small piece of wax and put it on a radiator to soften. Using a pocket knife, press wax into the holes. As soon as it hardens, scrape the repair flush with an old credit card. Fold a piece of sandpaper, and use the paper backing to burnish the wax filling.

ABRASIVES

The surfaces of wood must be brought to as near-perfect a finish as possible before beginning to apply varnish, lacquer, or any other clear coating. Rubbing wood smooth with abrasives is the usual way of getting the desired result, and woodworkers are today presented with an enormous choice of products to achieve their aims.

Not only is the wood itself smoothed with abrasives, but each coat of finish is also rubbed over lightly, to remove specks of dust and other debris that become embedded as the finish sets.

Although sandpaper as such is no longer manufactured, the term is still used to describe all forms of abrasive, and we still "sand" wood by hand and with power tools. Most abrasives are now manufactured using synthetic materials that are far superior to the sandpaper of old.

The structure of modern abrasives

An abrasive for woodworking is made by gluing irregular particles of natural or synthetic grit to a backing sheet, usually of paper or cloth. The efficiency, or the rate at which the abrasive wears away the wood, depends on several factors: the size of the particles and the ability of the material to retain its cutting edges; the degree to which the sandpaper can resist clogging with wood dust and sticky resins; and the quality of the bond between grit and backing, without which the particles become detached and are swept away.

Abrasive materials

You can choose from a number of abrasive grits, depending on their relative costs and the nature of the material you are finishing.

Crushed glass is used to make inexpensive abrasive paper, intended primarily for sanding softwood that is to be painted. When compared with other abrasives, glass is fairly soft and wears rapidly. Glasspaper can be recognized easily by its sandy color.

Garnet is a natural mineral which, when crushed, produces relatively hard particles with sharp cutting edges. It has the added advantage that the grains tend to fracture before they become dull, presenting fresh cutting edges—in effect, they are self-sharpening. Reddish-brown garnet paper is used by cabinetmakers for sanding softwoods and hardwoods.

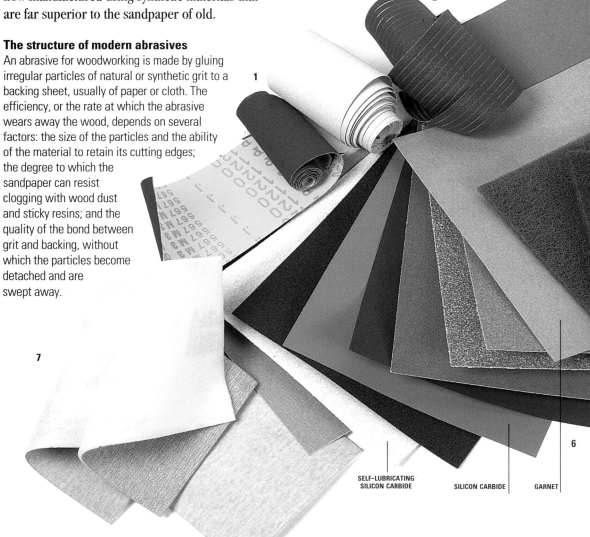

SELF-LUBRICATING
SILICON CARBIDE   SILICON CARBIDE   GARNET

Aluminum oxide is used to manufacture a great many abrasive products for sanding by hand and with power tools. Available in a number of different colors, aluminum oxide is especially suitable for sanding dense hardwoods to a fine finish.

Silicon carbide is the hardest and most expensive woodworking abrasive. It is an excellent material for sanding hardwoods, composite board and chipboard, but it is most often used for manufacturing abrasive paper and cloth for rubbing down between coats of varnish and paint. Water is used as a lubricant when smoothing finishes with black to dark-gray paper. A pale gray, self-lubricating paper is available for rubbing down finishes that would be harmed by water.

ALUMINUM-OXIDE

CRUSHED GLASS

1 Paper- or cloth-backed rolls
Economical and ideal for sanding turned legs and spindles.

2 Slashed cloths
They can be crumpled in the hand and applied to work on the lathe.

3 Velour-backed strips
Peel-off strips for sanding blocks and power sanders.

Backing
The backing is basically nothing more than a vehicle that carries the grit to the work. Nevertheless, the choice of backing material can be crucial to the performance of the abrasive.

Paper is the cheapest backing material used in the manufacture of woodworking abrasives. It is available in a range of thicknesses or "weights"—flexible lightweight papers are ideal for sanding by hand, although medium-weight backing is perhaps better for wrapping around a sanding block. Thicker papers are used with power sanders. Paper backings are designated by letter, according to their thickness or flexibility, ranging from A, the lightest, to F.

Cloth or woven-textile backings provide very tough and durable, yet flexible, abrasive products. You can crease a good cloth backing without cracking, splitting, or shedding its grit. Cloth makes ideal belts for power sanders and strips for smoothing turned spindles.

Nonwoven nylon-fiber pads, impregnated with aluminum-oxide or silicon-carbide grains, are ideal for rubbing down finishes and for applying wax polish and oil. The large cavities within the pad will not become clogged, and it can be washed out under running water. The abrasive coating extends throughout the thickness of a pad so that, as the fibers get worn away, fresh abrasive is exposed. Abrasive belts, rolls, and disks are all made with nylon-fiber backing.

Nylon fiber is frequently used for stripping old finishes, and because it does not rust, it is ideal for applying water-based products. Nylon-fiber pads are safe to use on oak, which is prone to staining when minute particles from steel wool get caught in its open grain.

Non-abrasive polishing pads make excellent applicators for wood dyes, oils, and wax polishes.

Foamed plastic is used as a secondary backing when you need to spread even pressure over a contoured surface. You can buy paper-backed silicon-carbide glued to thin sponges, for rubbing down varnished moldings, turned legs, or spindles.

4 Foam-backed pads
Flexible pads follow the contours of a workpiece.

5 Non-woven pads
Nylon fiber impregnated with abrasive material.

6 Standard-size sheets
Sandpaper or cloth sheets measure 11 x 9in (280 x 230mm).

7 Flexible-foam pads
Ideal for sanding mouldings.

Bond

The bond, or method of gluing abrasives to the backing, is vital, both in making sure the grit stays put, and because it affects the characteristics of sandpaper.

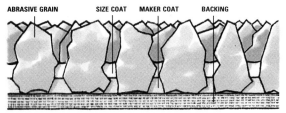

ABRASIVE GRAIN   SIZE COAT   MAKER COAT   BACKING

As the abrasive particles are embedded in the first, or maker, coat of adhesive, an electrostatic charge orientates each grain so that it stands perpendicular to the backing, with its sharp cutting edges uppermost. A second layer of adhesive, known as the size coat, is sprayed onto the abrasive to anchor the grains and provide lateral support.

Animal glue, which softens with heat generated by sanding, is used when flexibility is a requirement. Resin, on the other hand, is heat-resistant, making it ideal for power sanding. Because it is waterproof, resin is also used for the manufacture of waterproof abrasives. A combination of adhesives modifies the properties of a paper. Resin over glue, for example, would make a relatively heat-resistant paper that would be more flexible than a resin-over-resin mix.

Additives

A third coating of stearate, a powdered soap, packs the spaces between the grains, presenting a finer abrasive surface to the work and reducing premature clogging with wood dust. Stearate, and other chemical additives, act as dry lubricants for abrasives used for rubbing down coats of hard finish.

Antistatic additives in the size coat reduce clogging dramatically and increase the efficiency of dust extractors. This leads to a decrease in dust deposits on the work, surrounding surfaces, and power tools—a distinct advantage when you may have to sand work-pieces and apply finishes in the same workshop.

Storing abrasives

Wrap sandpaper or cloth in plastic to protect it from damp or humid conditions. Store sheets flat, and don't let the abrasive surfaces rub together.

GRADING SANDPAPER

Sandpapers are graded according to particle size, and are categorized as extra-fine, fine, medium, coarse, or extra-coarse. For most purposes, these classifications are adequate, but should you want to work through a series of precisely graded abrasives, each category is subdivided by number. There are several different grading systems in operation, none of which make for exact comparison. However, as the chart below demonstrates, you can safely assume that the higher the number, the finer the grit.

Sandpaper grades		
Extra-coarse	50	1
	60	½
Coarse	80	0
	100	2/0
Medium	120	3/0
	150	4/0
	180	5/0
Fine	220	6/0
	240	7/0
	280	8/0
Extra-fine	320	9/0
	360	-
	400	-
	500	-
	600	-

Closed or open coat

Sandpapers are also categorized according to the density of grit. A closed-coat sandpaper, with densely packed abrasive grains, cuts relatively quickly, as it has a great many cutting edges for a given area. An open-coat sandpaper has larger spaces between the grains, which reduces clogging and is more suitable for resinous softwoods.

SANDING BY HAND

Most woodworkers resort to power sanding in the early stages of preparing a workpiece, but it is usually necessary to finish by hand, especially if the work includes moldings. You can, of course, do the whole thing by hand—it just takes longer.

Always sand parallel to the grain, working from coarser to finer grits so that each application removes the scratches left by the previous paper or cloth. Stroking abrasives across the grain leaves scratches that are difficult to remove.

You will find it easier to sand most components before assembly, but take care not to round over the shoulders of a joint or create a slack fit by removing too much wood. Restoring old furniture presents additional problems of sanding up to corners and of possibly sanding across the grain where one component meets another.

Sanding flat surfaces
Stand beside the bench so that you can rub a sanding block in straight strokes, parallel with the grain; sweeping your arm in an arc tends to leave cross-grain scratches. Work at a steady pace, letting the abrasive do the work. It pays to change the paper frequently, rather than tiring yourself by rubbing harder to achieve the same ends.

Cover the surface evenly, keeping the block flat on the wood at all times, especially as you approach the edges of the work, or you may inadvertently round over sharp corners.

Sanding end grain
Before sanding, stroke end grain with your fingers to determine the direction of fiber growth. It will feel smoother in one direction than the other; to achieve the best finish, sand in the smoothest direction.

SANDING BLOCKS

It is much easier to sand a flat surface evenly if you wrap a piece of abrasive paper around a sanding block. You can make your own from a block of wood with a piece of cork tile glued to the underside, but this is hardly worth the trouble when factory-made cork or rubber sanding blocks are so cheap.

Most blocks are designed to be wrapped with a piece of sandpaper torn from a standard sheet, but you can buy sanding blocks that take ready-cut self-adhesive or velour-backed strips of abrasive that are peeled off when they need replacing. Double-sided blocks are made with firm plastic foam on one side, for sanding flat surfaces, and a softer sponge on the reverse, for moldings and curved profiles.

Velcro-lined foam plastic   **Double-sided**   **Cork**   **Rubber**

Tearing sandpaper
Fold a sheet of sandpaper over the edge of a bench, and tear it into strips that fit your sanding block. Wrap a piece of the paper around the sole of the block, gripping the sides with fingers and thumb.

Sanding small items
It is impossible to clamp and sand small items using conventional methods. Instead, glue a sheet of sandpaper face up on a flat board and rub the workpiece across the abrasive.

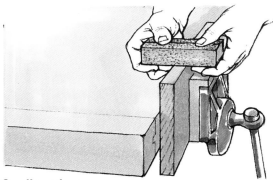

Sanding edges

It is even more difficult to retain sharp corners when sanding narrow edges. To keep the block level, clamp the work upright in a vise and, holding the block at each end, run your fingertips along each side of the work as you rub the abrasive back and forth. Finally, stroke the block lightly along the corner to remove the arris and prevent splinters.

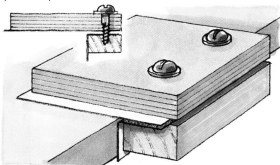

Making an edge-sanding block

It is especially important to sand edges accurately when working on edge-veneered boards. Screw together two pieces of wood to make an edge-sanding block, trapping two pieces of sandpaper face-to-face between them. Fold back one piece of paper to form a right angle. Rub the block along the edge of the work, simultaneously sanding both adjacent surfaces.

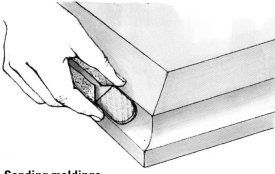

Sanding moldings

Wrap sandpaper around a shaped block or dowel when sanding moldings. Alternatively, use foam-backed paper or an impregnated nylon-fiber pad.

SANDING SEQUENCE

Every woodworker develops his or her preferred sequence for preparing a workpiece for finishing, but the following will serve as a guide to suitable grades of abrasive to achieve the result. You may need to experiment and modify the sequence when dealing with different woods. Sanding a close-grain hardwood with an extra-fine abrasive, for example, tends to burnish the surface, making it more difficult to apply wood dye subsequently.

Start with 120 grit aluminum-oxide or garnet paper followed by 180 grit, until the surface appears smooth and free from tool marks and similar blemishes. You only need to resort to anything as coarse as 80 to 100 grit if the wood is not already planed to a reasonably smooth surface.

Remove the dust between sandings, using a tack rag—a sticky cloth designed for picking up dust and fine debris. If you fail to keep the work clean, abrasive particles shed during the previous sanding may leave relatively deep scratches in the surface.

Sand again for no more than 30 to 60 seconds, using 220 grit, then raise the grain by wiping the surface with a damp cloth. Wait for 10 to 20 minutes, by which time the moisture will have caused the minute wood fibers to expand and stand up on the surface. Lightly skim the surface with a fresh piece of 220 abrasive to remove these "whiskers" leaving a perfectly smooth surface. It is particularly important to raise grain before applying water-based products.

At this stage, you can safely apply a surface finish, but if you feel the workpiece demands an extra-special finish, raise the grain once more and rub down very lightly, using 320 grit paper or an impregnated nylon-fiber pad.

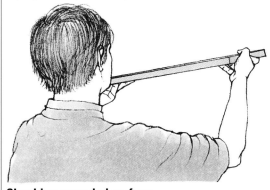

Checking a sanded surface

Inspect the workpiece against the light at a shallow angle, to check that the surface is sanded evenly and that you have removed all obvious scratches.

POWER SANDING

Nowadays, portable sanding machines relieve the woodworker from the tiresome chore of sanding for long periods, but even orbital sanders are apt to leave tiny whorls or scratches on the wood that show up only after the first coat of finish is applied. As a safeguard, raise the grain with a damp cloth after you have finished power sanding, and rub over lightly by hand, using a fine abrasive paper or nylon-fiber pad.

Belt sander

Belt sanders

These are heavy-duty power sanders that are capable of reducing even sawn lumber to a smooth finish. As a result, they remove a great deal of wood very quickly, and have to be carefully controlled to avoid rounding over the edges of a workpiece or wearing through a layer of veneer. Special accessories that frame the sanding bed are helpful in preventing the tool from tilting, especially as you approach the edge of a panel. Belt sanding creates a great deal of dust, so use a collecting bag or an extractor (see page 106).

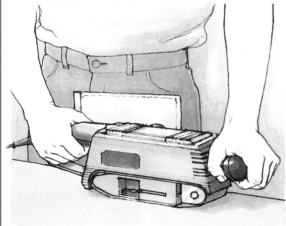

Sanding belts

Cloth- and paper-backed belts are made for the average 2⅜ to 4in (60 to 100mm) wide sanders. They are held taut between two rollers, the front one being adjustable to control tension and tracking. Operating a lever releases the tension so you can change a belt; once the sander is running, adjust a small knob to center the belt on the rollers. Use medium-to-fine abrasive belts for most applications.

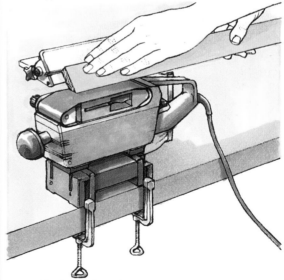

Using a belt sander

There are few occasions when you would need a belt sander for fine woodwork, but it is useful for smoothing large baulks of lumber or some man-made boards. Switch on and gradually lower the sander onto the work. As soon as you make contact, move the sander forward – allowing the tool to remain stationary or dropping it heavily onto the surface will score the wood deeply. Sand in the direction of the grain only, keeping the tool moving and using parallel overlapping strokes. Lift the sander off the work before switching off.

Fixed belt sanders

Using a purpose-made clamp, you can attach a portable belt sander upside-down on a bench, allowing you to sand small components by applying them to the moving belt. You can use a fence to guide the work, and you can shape curved workpieces over the end roller.

Orbital sanders

Provided you work through a series of progressively finer abrasives (see page 102) and take the trouble to raise the grain before the final light sanding, an orbital sander will produce a surface that, to all intents and purposes, is ready for finishing. Before applying a clear finish, however, always inspect the surface carefully to make sure there are no swirling scratches caused by the elliptical motion of the base plate. Some orbital sanders can be switched to a straight reciprocal stroke to eliminate this possibility.

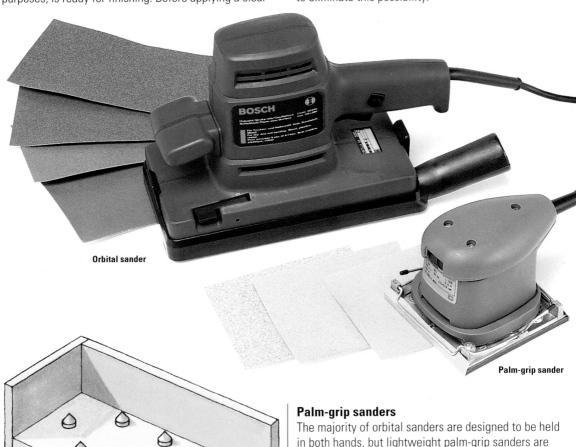

Orbital sander

Palm-grip sander

Palm-grip sanders

The majority of orbital sanders are designed to be held in both hands, but lightweight palm-grip sanders are also available.

Sanding sheets

Strips of sandpaper are made specifically for use with orbital sanders. Designated as half, third, and quarter sheets, their proportions are based on the standard-size sheets made for hand-sanding (see page 99). They are held in place by a wire clamp at each end of the sander's base plate; alternatively, strips are velour-lined or self-adhesive for easy replacement. To preserve your health and reduce clogging, choose a sander that incorporates dust extraction; the base plate and sandpaper are both perforated so that dust is sucked directly from under the tool into a collecting bag or vacuum cleaner (see page 106).

Perforating sandpaper

Ready-made sheets are very convenient, but you can make considerable cost savings by perforating plain sandpaper strips or rolls. Using a soft pencil and white paper, make a rubbing of the perforations in your sander's base plate. Use it as a pattern for drilling matching holes in a board, and glue into them short lengths of pointed dowel rod.

Attach a strip of abrasive to the base plate, and then press your sander down onto your perforator to pierce the sandpaper.

Using orbital sanders

Don't apply excessive pressure to an orbital sander, as this tends to overheat the abrasive, causing dust and resin to clog the grit prematurely. A sensation of pins and needles in your fingers after prolonged sanding indicates that you are pressing too hard.

Keep the tool moving back and forth with the grain, covering the surface as evenly as possible. If you are using a variable-speed sander, select the slowest rate for coarser grits and gradually increase the speed as you progress with finer abrasives.

Cordless sanders

There are obvious advantages to be gained from using a battery-powered sander: there's no electrical cord to get caught up on the workpiece, and you can work outside if you wish, completely independent of a socket. However, only a few cordless sanders are currently available.

RANDOM-ORBITAL SANDERS

The combined rotational and eccentric motions of a random-orbital sander practically eliminate discernible scratches on a wood surface. The circular base plate takes sanding disks, along with the usual options—velcro or self-adhesive attachment, and perforations for dust extraction. Some sanders can cope with flat and curved surfaces, while others have interchangeable base plates so you can increase the sanding area for working on large boards or panels. The only disadvantage is that you cannot sand into corners (see left).

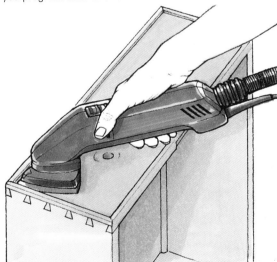

Sanding into corners

With a well-designed orbital sander, it should be possible to sand into right angles and up to the ends of fixed rails or panels. However, for really tight corners and cross-grain miters, use a delta sander, which has a triangular base plate.

Disk sanders

With the exception of bench-mounted machines, cabinetmakers seldom use disk sanders, which can score deep scratches in the wood. However, wood-turners employ the combined actions of disk sander and lathe to their advantage for sanding bowls and platters.

Flexible-shaft sanders and disks

Arbor-mounted foam pads, from 1 to 3in (25 to 75mm) in diameter, are made for use in portable power drills or, better still, highly maneuverable, flexible-shaft sanders. Velour-lined or self-adhesive abrasive disks, with cloth or paper backing, come ready-made to fit every size of foam pad.

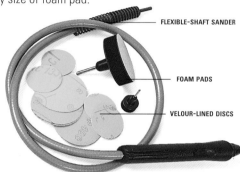

FLEXIBLE-SHAFT SANDER

FOAM PADS

VELOUR-LINED DISCS

Advantages for woodturners

Miniature disk sanders are ideal for intricate woodwork such as carving or modelmaking, but they are especially suited to woodturners, because the soft-foam pads conform to the changing contours of a wooden bowl or vase, providing an even distribution of pressure without generating too much heat. More importantly, since both the disk and workpiece rotate simultaneously, you can remove tool marks rapidly without scratching the wood.

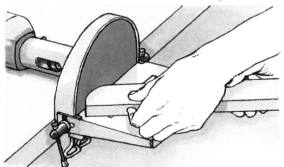

Bench-mounted sanders

A relatively large-diameter metal disk sander, mounted rigidly on the bench, is perfect for finishing end grain. Using coarse to fine grits, you can also shape work-pieces with a disk sander. Keep the workpiece moving, and press the end grain lightly against the downward-rotating side of the disk. Applying excessive pressure invariably scorches the wood.

PROTECTING YOURSELF FROM DUST

Power sanders are not especially dangerous, provided they are used with care. However, the dust generated by sanding can be very injurious to health and may also constitute a fire hazard.

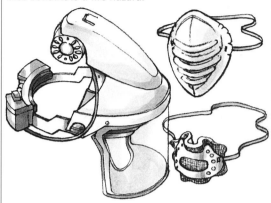

Face masks and helmets

At the very least, make sure you wear a face mask to cover your nose and mouth when sanding. Cheap disposable masks are available from any tool store and are usually supplied as part of the kit when you rent power sanders.

A battery-powered respirator, built into a light-weight helmet, offers the best protection. A stream of filtered air, blown behind the transparent face screen, prevents you from breathing airborne dust.

Dust extractors

Good-quality power sanders have an extractor port that discharges dust into a bag, for disposal after work or when the bag is full. For greater efficiency, attach a sander to an industrial vacuum cleaner that sucks the dust directly from the work surface. A purpose-made extractor is activated as you switch on the sander.

SCRAPING WOOD

Even though sanding is the most-used method for smoothing wood, scraping the surface, which removes minute shavings instead of dust particles, produces a superior finish. Because a scraper can take such a fine cut, you can use it on areas of wild grain that are difficult to plane well.

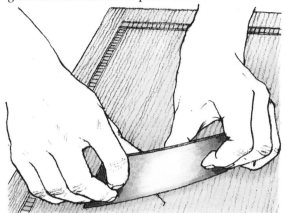

Controlling a cabinet scraper
Holding the scraper in both hands, lean it away from you and push the tool forward. Bending a scraper, by pressing with your thumbs near the bottom edge, concentrates the forces in a narrow band, so that you can scrape small blemishes from the wood. By experimenting with different curvatures and angles, you can vary the action and cutting depth to suit the particular task.

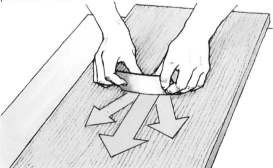

Leveling wood panels
To scrape a panel flat and level, work in two directions at a slight angle to the general direction of grain. To finish, smooth the wood by scraping parallel with the grain. Use a similar method when scraping out small patches of dried glue or scorching, to avoid leaving a deep hollow.

Cabinet scrapers
The standard cabinet scraper is nothing more than a small rectangle of tempered steel. For shaped surfaces and moldings, you need a scraper with a pair of curved edges, or a goose-neck scraper that is shaped to accommodate a great many convex and concave radii. Before using a scraper, you must prepare and sharpen its cutting edges.

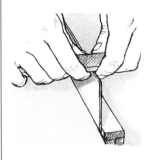

1 Filing a scraper
Clamp the scraper in a bench vise and draw-file its two long edges to make them perfectly square. To prevent the file from rocking, try running your fingertips against each face of the scraper.

2 Honing the scraper
Filing leaves rough edges that must be rubbed down with an oiled slipstone. Keep the stone flat on the faces of the scraper, and rub it along both sides of each cutting edge.

3 Raising a burr
Stretch the metal along both cutting edges with a smooth metal burnisher. If you can't get the proper tool, use the curved back of a gouge. Holding the scraper on the bench top, strop each edge firmly four or five times, drawing the burnisher toward you while keeping it flat on the scraper.

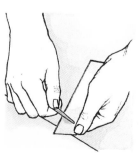

4 Turning the burr
For the scraper to function, the raised burrs must be folded over at right angles. Holding the burnisher at a slight angle to the burred edge, draw the tool firmly along the scraper two or three times.

FILLING AND SEALING GRAIN

An open-grain lumber, such as oak or ash, looks good coated with satin varnish or oil, but when French polish or gloss varnish sinks into each pore, the result is a speckled, pitted surface that detracts from the quality of the finish.

Perhaps the ideal solution is to apply coat after coat of the finish itself, rubbing down between applications until the pores are filled flush, but this is a slow, laborious process, which is why the majority of woodworkers opt for a ready-mixed grain filler. Most general-purpose fillers are thick wood-color pastes. Choose a color that closely resembles the species you are finishing, always erring on the darker side when a perfect match is impossible.

1 Applying grain filler
Make sure the surface is completely clean and dust-free. Dip a pad of coarse burlap into the grain filler and rub it vigorously into the wood, using over-lapping circular strokes.

2 Removing excess filler
Before the paste dries completely, wipe across the grain with clean burlap to remove excess filler from the surface. Use a pointed stick to remove paste embedded in moldings or carving.

3 Rubbing down
Leave the grain filler to dry thoroughly overnight, then sand lightly in the direction of the grain, using 220 grit, self-lubricating silicon-carbide paper. Rub moldings or turned pieces with an abrasive nylon-fiber pad.

Filling stained wood
It is debatable whether it is better to color the wood before or after grain filling. To fill first may result in patchy, uneven color, but if you apply filler over stained wood, there is the possibility that you may wear through the color when sanding at a later stage. One solution is to stain the wood first, then protect it with sanding sealer, or two coats of transparent French polish, before applying a grain filler mixed with some of the same compatible wood dye.

SANDING SEALER
Sealing serves more than one purpose. On porous woods it prevents the finish from being absorbed, just as a primer does for paint, and can be used as the first base coat for French polish. Perhaps most important of all, shellac-based sanding sealer makes an excellent barrier coat, preventing wood stains from being redissolved and also sealing in contaminants, such as silicone oil, that affect the setting of the final finish. For this reason, it often makes sense to seal old furniture that has been stripped prior to refinishing. However, since sanding sealer prevents some varnishes from setting satisfactorily, check the manufacturer's directions before starting.

Applying sanding sealer
Sand the work well and pick up the dust with a tack rag. Brush sanding sealer onto the wood and leave it to dry for an hour or two. Rub the surface with fine sandpaper, an abrasive pad, or 0000-grade steel wool before applying your chosen finish. You may need a second sealing coat on very porous wood.

BLEACHING WOOD

Woodworkers often resort to bleaching in order to obliterate staining. For this, you should use a comparatively mild bleach, such as a solution of oxalic acid. However, it may also be desirable to reduce the depth of color of a workpiece, perhaps so you can stain it to resemble a different species, or maybe to stain several components the same color. To alter the color of wood drastically, you need a strong two-part commercial bleach. This is usually sold in kit form, comprising a pair of clearly labeled plastic bottles, one containing an alkali and the other hydrogen peroxide. However, the bottles may be labeled A and B, or 1 and 2.

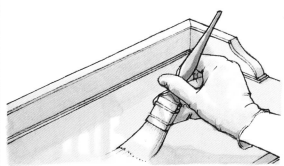

1 Applying solution A
Pour some of the contents of bottle A into a glass or plastic container and, using a white-fibre or nylon brush, wet the workpiece evenly. Don't splash bleach onto adjacent surfaces, and if you have to work on a vertical surface, start at the bottom to keep runs from streaking the surface.

2 Applying solution B
About 5 to 10 minutes later, during which time the wood may darken, use a different brush to apply the second solution. The chemical reaction causes foaming on the surface of the wood.

Testing the effectiveness of bleach
Because some woods bleach better than others, it is worth testing a sample before you treat the workpiece itself. As a rough guide, ash, beech, elm, and sycamore are easy to bleach, whereas you may have to bleach other woods, such as mahogany, rosewood, oak, and padauk, a second time to get the color you want.

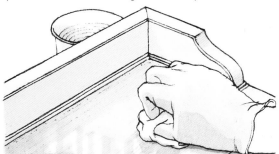

3 Neutralizing the bleach
When it is dry, or as soon as the wood is the desired color, neutralize the bleach by washing the work with a weak acetic-acid solution, comprising one teaspoon of white vinegar in a pint of water. Put the work aside for about three days, then sand down the raised grain and apply the finish.

SAFETY PRECAUTIONS
Wood bleach is a dangerous substance which must be handled with care and stored in the dark, out of the reach of children.

- Wear protective gloves, goggles, and an apron.

- Wear a face mask when sanding wood that has been bleached.

- Ventilate the workshop or work outside.

- Have a supply of water handy so that you can rinse your skin immediately if you splash yourself with bleach. If you are going to work outside, fill a bucket with water.

- If you get bleach in your eyes, rinse well with running water and seek medical attention.

- Never mix the two solutions except on the wood, and always apply them with separate brushes. Discard any unused bleach.

STAINING WOOD

A wood stain or dye is fundamentally different from a surface finish such as paint or varnish. Paint, which colors the wood by depositing a relatively dense layer of pigments on the surface, also forms a protective coating on the workpiece, and clear varnish is essentially a paint without the colored pigments. A true penetrating dye or stain soaks into the wood, taking the color deep into the fibers. However, it provides no protection at all, and so a clear finish is always applied to a stained workpiece afterward.

Modern stains often contain translucent pigments that lodge in the pores of the wood, accentuating the grain. However, without thorough testing, it can be difficult to determine which ready-made stains contain pigments because a manufacturer may create a whole line of stains, only some of which contain pigments to create particular colors. Successive applications of a pigmented stain gradually darken the wood, whereas applying more than one coat of a non-pigmented stain has little effect on the color.

1 Solvent or oil stains
2 Acrylic stains
3 Denatured alcohol
4 Ready-mixed water stains
5 Mineralspirits
6 Ready-mixed spirit stains
7 Concentrated water stains
8 Powdered water stains

Solvent or oil stains

The most widely available penetrating stains, made from oil-soluble dyes, are thinned with mineral spirits. Known as solvent stains or oil stains, these wood dyes are easy to apply evenly, will not raise the grain, and dry relatively quickly. Oil stains are made in a wide range of woodlike colors, which you can mix to achieve intermediate shades. Some solvent stains contain translucent pigments that make them fade-resistant.

Spirit stains

Traditional spirit stains are made by dissolving aniline dyes in denatured alcohol. The main disadvantage with spirit stains is their extremely rapid drying time, which makes it difficult to get even coverage without leaving darker patches of overlapping color. Some manufacturers supply ready-mixed stains, and they are also available in powder form which you can mix with alcohol and a little thinned shellac as a binder. Concentrated powder stains, which come in a limited choice of strong colors, are used mainly for tinting French polish.

Water stains

Water stains are available from specialists as ready-made wood-color dyes. You can also buy them as crystals or powders for dissolving in hot water so you can mix any color you want. Water stains dry slowly, which means there is plenty of time to achieve an even distribution of color, but you must allow adequate time for the water to evaporate completely before you apply a finish. They also raise the grain, leaving a rough surface, so it is essential to wet the wood and sand down prior to applying water stains (see page 102).

Acrylic stains

The latest generation of water stains, based on acrylic resins, are emulsions that leave a film of color on the surface of the wood. They raise the grain less than traditional water stains and are more resistant to fading. In addition to the usual woodlike colors, acrylic stains are made in a choice of pastel shades; it can, however, be difficult to predict the final color produced by these pastel-colored stains on dark hardwoods. All acrylic stains need to be diluted by about 10 percent when used on dense hardwoods.

COMPATIBILITY

You can create practically any color you like by mixing compatible wood stains or dyes, and you can reduce the strength of a color by adding more of the relevant solvent. However, you should guard against overlaying a penetrating stain, even one that has dried out, with a surface finish that contains a similar solvent. As you drag a brush or pad across the surface, the solvent may reactivate the color, causing it to bleed into the surface finish.

As a basic rule, select a stain that will not react with the finish you want to apply, or seal the stain first to prevent solvent from disturbing the color. It is always worth testing the stain and finish before applying either to a workpiece.

Solvent stains

Seal a solvent stain (oil stain) with shellac or sanding sealer before applying a varnish, lacquer, or wax polish that is thinned with mineral spirits, turpentine, or cellulose thinner.

Spirit stains

You can use a spirit stain under any finish, except for French polish. When the stained surface is completely dry, gently wipe it with a clean rag before applying a finish.

Water and acrylic stains

Allow a stain thinned with water to dry for 48 hours before overlaying with a solvent-based finish—any moisture that has not evaporated can cause the finish to develop a white haze or milkiness. Although a dry water stain should not react with a water-based finish, always test the finish in an inconspicuous place before you apply it.

If you forget to raise the grain before applying a water stain (see page 102), rub the stained surface very lightly with 220 grit abrasive paper, and then pick up the dust with a tack rag before applying any finish.

APPLYING PENETRATING STAINS

Wet the surface to get some idea of what a particular workpiece will look like under a clear finish, and if in doubt, apply some of the actual finish you intend to use. If you are unhappy with its depth of color, or if you feel it doesn't quite match another piece of wood you are working with, take a scrap piece of the same wood and make a test strip to try out a stain before coloring the workpiece itself (see opposite).

Setting up for staining

Plan the work sequence in advance, to minimize the possibility of stain running onto adjacent surfaces or one area of color drying before you can "pick up" the wet edges. If you have to color both sides of a work-piece, stain the least important side first, immediately wiping off any dye that runs over the edges.

Staining large panels

If possible, set up the workpiece so the surface to be stained is horizontal. Lay a large panel or door on a pair of sawhorses so that you can approach it from all sides.

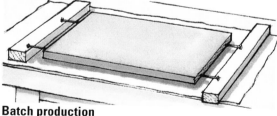

Batch production

It is sometimes convenient to stain components before assembly, setting them aside to dry while you complete the batch.

To color a number of adjustable bookshelves, for example, drive a pair of nails or screws into each end. Lay each shelf on a bench, with the nails or screws resting on strips of wood to raise the shelf off the work surface. Having stained each side in turn, stand the shelf on end against a wall until the stain is dry.

Applicators

You can use good-quality paintbrushes, decorators' paint pads covered with mohair pile, non-abrasive polishing pads (see page 99), or a pad of soft cloth to apply penetrating stains. You can also spray wood dyes, provided you have adequate extraction facilities. Wear heavy rubber gloves and old clothes or an apron when applying wood stains.

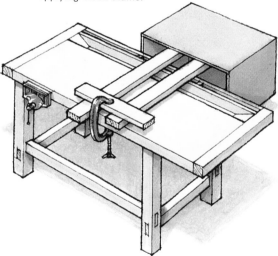

Supporting drawers and cabinets

After staining the inside of drawers or small cabinets, support them at a comfortable working height to complete the job, using cantilevered strips of wood clamped or screwed temporarily to a bench.

Preparing a workpiece for staining

Sand the workpiece well (see pages 101—6), making sure there are no scratches or defects that will absorb more stain than the surrounding wood. In addition, scrape off any patches of dried glue that could affect the absorption of stain.

Staining a flat surface

Pour enough stain to color the entire workpiece into a shallow dish. Brush or swab the stain onto the wood in the direction of the grain, blending in the wet edges before the dye has time to dry. When you have covered the surface, use a clean cloth pad to mop up excess stain, distributing it evenly across the workpiece. If you splash stain onto the wood, blend it in quickly to prevent a patchy appearance.

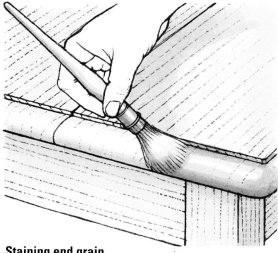

Staining end grain

Exposed end grain appears darker than the rest of the workpiece because the orientation of the cells allows it to absorb more penetrating stain. Painting the end grain with a coat of white shellac or sanding sealer will reduce the amount of color taken up by the wood. Alternatively, you can use thinned varnish, but you should wait 24 hours before you stain the wood.

MAKING A TEST STRIP

Before you color an actual workpiece, make a test strip to see how the wood will be affected by the stain you intend to use. It is important that the test strip is sanded as smooth as the workpiece you will be staining, because coarsely sanded wood absorbs more dye and will therefore appear darker than the same piece of wood prepared with a finer sandpaper.

Apply a coat of stain and let it dry. As a general rule, stains dry lighter than they appear when wet. Apply a second coat to see if it darkens the wood, leaving part of the first application exposed for comparison. If you apply more than two full coats of stain, the colour may become patchy due to uneven absorption of the liquid.

A second coat of a nonpigmented stain may not change the color appreciably, but you can modify it by overlaying with a compatible stain of a different color.

Once the stain is completely dry, paint one half of the test strip with the intended finish to see how it affects the color of the stain.

Test strip, using pigmented stain

Test strip, using nonpigmented stain

Coloring veneer

You can treat modern veneered panels like solid wood. However, old furniture was invariably veneered using water-soluble animal glue, and it would pay to use a spirit or solvent stain to color such items.

You can stain veneer patches or pieces of marquetry before gluing them in place. Dipping scraps of veneer in a dish of wood dye insures even coloring.

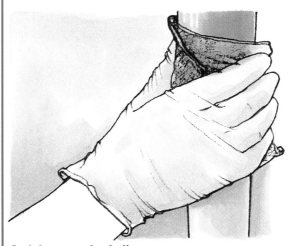

Staining turned spindles

Apply stain to turned legs and spindles with a rag or a nonwoven polishing pad. Rub the dye well into turned beads and fluting, then cup the applicator around the leg or spindle and rub it lengthwise.

Since turned work exposes end grain, it is very difficult to obtain even coverage.

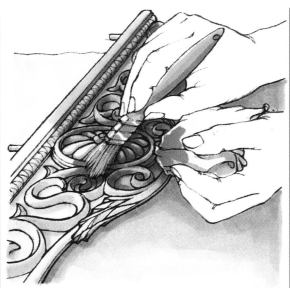

Staining carved work

Use a soft brush to apply penetrating stain to carving or intricate moldings, absorbing surplus stain immediately with rag or a paper towel.

STAINING SOFTWOOD

It is advisable to apply stain to softwood with a cloth pad rather than a paintbrush; highly absorbent wood tends to draw extra stain from a heavily loaded brush at the first point of contact, thus creating a patch of darker color.

The different rates of absorption between early-wood and latewood often give stained softwood a distinctly striped appearance. With some colors, this can be very attractive, but if it doesn't suit your requirements, try coloring the wood with varnish stain or dark-colored wax.

Softwood coloured with penetrating stain (left) and varnish stain

MODIFYING THE COLOR

No matter how practiced you become at judging colors and mixing dyes, inevitably there comes a time when the dried stain is not quite the color you had in mind. If it's too dark, you may be able to remove some stain, but don't make the mistake of trying to alter the color by applying layer upon layer of dye—this will simply lead to muddy colors or poor finish adhesion. Instead, add washes of tinted finish to modify the color gradually.

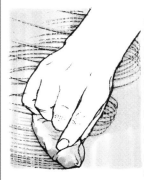

Adding tinted shellac
If the wood is to be French-polished, dissolve some powdered stain in denatured alcohol and add it to pale shellac. Apply a coat of the tinted shellac and let it dry. Keep adding washes of shellac, adjusting the color with spirit stain, until you achieve the right shade.

Applying tinted varnish
If you plan to varnish the workpiece, you can apply a sealer coat of tinted shellac. Alternatively, use a thinned wash of varnish stain, or add diluted wood dye to a compatible clear varnish. Gradually build up to the required tone with a series of thin coats, then apply a protective coat of full-strength varnish.

Toning with wax
If the color match is still not perfect, you can finally tip the balance by adding a dressing of colored wax. Rub on the wax in the direction of the grain, using an abrasive nylon pad or very fine steel wool; then buff it to a satin finish with a soft cloth.

Removing color
If a solvent-stained workpiece dries streaky or too dark in tone, wet the surface with mineral spirits and rub it with an abrasive nylon pad. Wipe the surface with a cloth to lift some of the stain and redistribute the remainder more evenly. At this stage, you can modify the color of the wood by applying another, paler stain while the wood is still damp.

ACCENTUATING MOLDINGS AND CARVING

You can bring a workpiece to life by using color to add depth to carving and intricate moldings. The process imitates the effects of natural wear, adding considerably to the appeal of antique or reproduction furniture and picture frames.

Highlighting
The simplest method is to wipe color from the high points while the stain is wet. Alternatively, sand these areas lightly with an abrasive pad after the stain has dried, and wash off the dust, using a cloth dampened with solvent.

Shading
You can add depth to the most delicate of raised patterns, using dark stain mixed into diluted French polish (see left). Seal the stained surface, then paint tinted shellac liberally onto carved and molded areas of the workpiece, allowing it to flow into all the nooks and crannies. Wipe the color off high points immediately, using a soft cloth, and let the shellac dry before applying a clear finish.

A FINISH FOR EVERY SITUATION

At one time, the terms lacquer and varnish were used to describe specific finishes. Lacquer was for the most part a clear coating that dried quickly by evaporation of the solvent, whereas a conventional varnish was a mixture of resins, oil, and solvent that dried by a combination of evaporation and oxidation. Nowadays, a great many finishes are so complex that they no longer fit exactly into either category, but manufacturers have continued to use the familiar terms so as not to disorientate their customers. As a consequence, the labels lacquer and varnish have become interchangeable; to avoid further confusion, the terms used here are those that you are most likely to encounter when buying wood finishes.

The bulk of varnishes and lacquers are clear to amber-colored finishes, designed primarily to protect the wood and accentuate its natural grain pattern. There are also modified finishes that contain colored dyes or pigments.

Clear polyurethane varnish is a tough and attractive finish for all interior wood surfaces

APPLYING VARNISH

There are no special skills to master when applying solvent-based or acrylic varnishes. However, a few basic procedures can help avoid some of the less obvious pitfalls.

Varnishing a flat panel

Supporting a large panel horizontally on a pair of trestles makes varnishing marginally easier, but there are few problems with finishing a hinged door or fixed panel, provided you guard against the varnish running.

1 Applying a sealer coat of oil varnish

Thin oil varnish by about 10 percent when applying a first sealer coat to bare wood. You can brush it onto the wood, but some woodworkers prefer to rub it into the grain with a soft cloth.

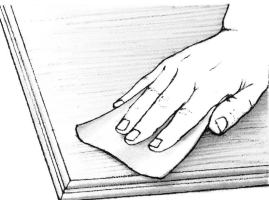

2 Rubbing down the first coat

Leave the sealer coat to harden overnight, then hold the work in a good source of light to inspect the varnished surface. Rub it down lightly in the direction of the grain, using fine waterproof paper dipped in water. Wipe the surface clean, using a cloth moistened with mineral spirits, and dry it with a paper towel.

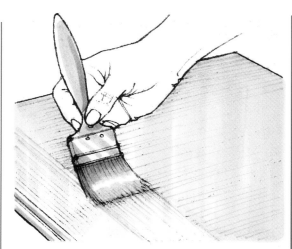

3 Brushing full-strength varnish

Paint oil varnish onto the wood, brushing first with the grain, then across it to spread the finish evenly. Always brush toward the area you have just finished, to blend the wet edges. It pays to work at a fairly brisk pace; varnish begins to set after about 10 minutes, and re-brushing it tends to leave permanent brushmarks. Finally "lay off" along the grain with very light strokes, using just the tips of the bristles to leave a smoothly varnished surface. When varnishing vertical surfaces, lay off with upward strokes of the brush.

Two full-strength coats of oil varnish should be adequate; for a perfect finish, rub down lightly between each hardened coat.

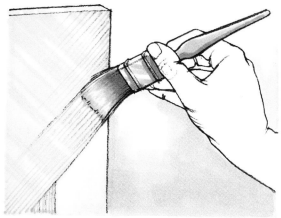

Varnishing edges

As you approach the edges of a panel, brush outward away from the center. If you flex the bristles back against the sharp arris, you will cause varnish to dribble down the edge.

It is best to blend in the edges of a workpiece as the work progresses, but if that proves troublesome, try varnishing the edges of a panel first and letting them dry. When you coat the flat surfaces, wipe runs from the edges with a rag.

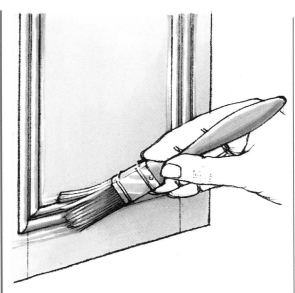

Varnishing moldings

Flexing a brush across a molding usually causes a teardrop of varnish to run down the surface. Avoid this by brushing along the molding only.

When finishing a paneled door, varnish the moldings first and then varnish the panel, brushing out from each corner toward the center.

Matting a gloss varnish

Matt and satin oil varnishes have very finely textured surfaces that serve to scatter the light. These look perfect, but you can achieve a smoother-feeling surface on components such as wooden chair arms or a table top by rubbing down a gloss varnish to a flat finish.

Rub the varnish with 000-grade steel wool dipped in wax polish. Leave the wax to harden, then burnish it with a soft cloth.

APPLYING ACRYLIC VARNISH

Many of the techniques employed when applying oil varnish are just as relevant to the application of acrylic varnish. The aim is still to acquire a flat, even coating without runs or brushmarks, but the chemical properties of acrylic varnish make it behave slightly differently from oil varnish.

Grain-raising characteristics

When a piece of wood absorbs water, its fibers swell and stand up above the surface. Because it is water-based, acrylic varnish has the same effect, making the final finish less than perfect. The solution is either to wet the wood first, and sand it smooth before applying acrylic varnish (see page 102), or to sand the first coat of varnish with fine waterproof paper dipped in water before recoating the work. Wipe up the dust with a cloth dampened with water; a tack rag may leave oily deposits that will spoil the next coat of acrylic varnish.

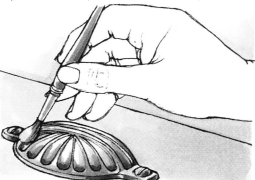

Problems with rust

Applying any water-based finish over unprotected steel or iron hardware, including wood screws and nails, will cause them to rust. Either remove metal hardware before you varnish the work, or protect them with a coat of de-waxed transparent shellac.

Don't use steel wool to rub acrylic varnish; tiny slivers of metal that get caught in the grain may rust, creating black spots on the wood. Use copper wool or an abrasive nylon-fiber pad (see page 99).

Applying the varnish

Acrylic varnish must be applied liberally, first by brushing across the grain, then laying off evenly as described for applying oil varnish.

Acrylic varnish dries in only 20 to 30 minutes, so you need to work fast, especially on a hot day, to avoid leaving permanent brushmarks in the finish.

You can apply a second coat after two hours. A total of three coats is enough for maximum protection.

APPLYING COLD-CURE LACQUER

This is a very different finish from conventional varnish. Although cold-cure lacquer is no more difficult to apply, it is important to be aware of how the curing process can be affected by inadequate preparation and inappropriate procedures.

Mixing cold-cure lacquer

Mix recommended amounts of hardener and lacquer in a glass jar or hard plastic container. Metal containers and some plastics may react with the hardener, preventing the lacquer from curing.

Once mixed, some cold-cure lacquers are usable for about three days. However, you can extend the pot life to about a week by covering the jar with plastic wrap, held in place with a rubber band. This type of lacquer will last even longer if you keep the sealed container, clearly marked, in a refrigerator.

Brush care

Apply cold-cure lacquer with any good-quality paintbrush. It can also be sprayed and can even be applied to large areas with a plastic-foam paint roller.

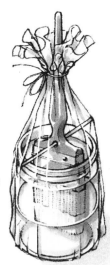

Once polymerization is complete, cold-cure lacquer becomes insoluble, so wash brushes in special lacquer thinner as soon as the work is complete. The brush can be left suspended in the mixed lacquer between coats, provided the whole container, including the brush, is sealed in plastic wrap.

Preparing the surface

As with any wood finish, the work must be smooth and clean; remove every trace of wax, which might prevent the lacquer curing. Any wood dye applied to the work must be compatible with the acid catalyst in the lacquer, so check the manufacturers' recommendations before coloring the wood.

Applying cold-cure lacquer

Adequate ventilation is important, especially when you are lacquering a floor, but keep the workshop warm.

Brush on lacquer liberally, using a flowing action and blending in wet edges as you go. Apply it relatively thickly, taking care to avoid runs or sagging.

The lacquer will be touch dry in about 15 minutes; apply a second coat after about an hour. If a third coat is required, apply it the following day.

There is no need to rub down between coats, except to correct blemishes. It you use stearated abrasives (see page 100), wipe the sanded surface with special lacquer thinner.

Modifying the finish

To achieve a perfect gloss finish, let the last coat harden for a few days, then sand it smooth with waterproof paper and water until the surface appears matt all over; a shiny patch indicates a hollow. Using a burnishing cream on a slightly damp cloth, buff the surface to a high gloss, and then rub it with a cloth.

To create a satin finish, rub the hardened lacquer with 000-grade steel wool lubricated with wax polish. Use coarser steel wool for a flat finish.

WAX POLISHES

Making wax polish from basic ingredients is sometimes advocated by traditionalists, but since there is such a variety of excellent polishes readily available, there seems little point in introducing a complication into what is otherwise one of the simplest of wood-finishing processes. Most commercially prepared wax polishes are a blend of relatively soft beeswax and hard carnauba wax, reduced to a usable consistency with turpentine or mineral spirits.

A traditional wax finish gives a sympathetic patina to a Georgian-style dressing table and chair

Paste wax polish

The most familiar form of wax polish is sold as a thick paste, packed in flat cans or foil containers. Paste wax, applied with a cloth pad or fine steel wool, serves as an ideal dressing over another finish.

Liquid wax polish

When you want to wax a large area of oak paneling, for example, it is probably easiest to brush on liquid wax polish that has the consistency of cream.

Floor wax

Floor wax is a liquid polish formulated for hardwearing surfaces. It is usually available as a clear polish only.

Tinted brushing polish deepens the color of pine furniture

Silicones

Silicone oil, which is added to some polishes to make them easier to apply and burnish, will repel most surface coatings should the piece require refinishing in the future. Sealing the wood beforehand is a wise precaution, but applying a chemical stripper at a later date may still allow silicone oil to penetrate the pores. You should therefore decide from the beginning whether it would be better to finish a piece with a silicone-free wax polish.

Woodturning sticks

Carnauba wax is the main ingredient for sticks that are hard enough to be used as a friction polish on work-pieces being turned in a lathe.

Colored polish

White to pale-yellow polishes do not alter the color of the wood to a great extent, but there is also an extensive choice of darker shades, sometimes referred to as staining waxes, that can be used to modify the color of a workpiece and to hide scratches and minor blemishes. Dark-brown to black polish is a popular finish for oak furniture; it enhances the patina of old wood and, by lodging in the open pores, accentuates the grain pattern. There are warm golden-brown polishes, made to put the color back into stripped pine, and orange-red polishes to enrich faded mahogany. Applying one polish over another creates even more subtle shades and tints.

It is not a good idea to wax chairs or benches with dark-colored polishes in case your body heat should soften the wax and stain your clothing. The same goes for finishing the insides of drawers; long-term contact could discolor delicate fabrics.

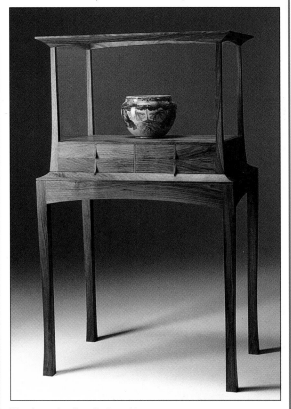

Wax-dressed walnut display cabinet

APPLYING WAX POLISHES

Finishing wood with a wax polish could hardly be simpler, since it requires only careful application and enough energy to burnish the surface to a deep shine. However, as with any wood finish, the workpiece must be sanded smooth and any blemishes filled or repaired before you can achieve a satisfactory result (see pages 96—108). Wipe the surface with mineral spirits to remove traces of grease and old wax polish.

Although there is no need to fill the grain, it is always best to seal the work with two coats of French polish or sanding sealer before applying wax polish, especially if you have colored the wood with solvent stain. Rub down the sealer coats with fine silicon-carbide paper.

WAX-POLISHING BRUSHES

Professional wood finishers sometimes use a bristle brush to burnish hardened wax polish. You can use a clean shoe brush, but you might want to buy a purpose-made furniture brush with a handle to keep your knuckles out of the way when burnishing into awkward corners and recesses. In addition, there are circular brushes designed to fit the chuck of a power drill; when you are using one of these, apply light pressure only and keep the brush moving across the polished surface.

HAND BRUSH FOR WAX POLISH

DRILL BRUSH

SHOE BRUSH

FURNITURE BRUSH

1 Applying paste wax polish

Dip a cloth pad in paste wax and apply the first coat, using overlapping circular strokes to rub the wax into the grain. Cover the surface evenly, then finish by rubbing in the direction of the grain. If the polish proves difficult to spread, warm the can on a radiator.

2 Building up a layer of polish

After about 15 to 20 minutes, use 000-grade steel wool or an abrasive nylon pad to rub on more wax polish, this time working along the grain. Put the work aside for 24 hours so the solvent can evaporate. On new work, apply four or five coats of wax in all, allowing each one to harden overnight.

3 Burnishing the polish

When the wax has hardened thoroughly, burnish it vigorously with a soft cloth pad. Some polishers prefer to use a furniture brush because it raises a better shine, particularly when burnishing carved work. Finally, rub over all polished surfaces with a clean soft cloth.

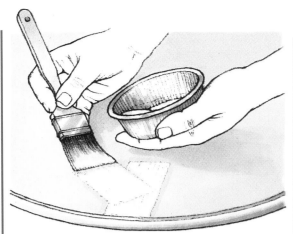

1 Brushing liquid wax polish
Decant some polish into a shallow dish and brush it liberally onto the wood, spreading the wax as evenly as possible. Let the solvent evaporate for about an hour.

2 Applying subsequent coats
Apply a second coat of wax with a soft cloth pad. Use circular strokes at first, and finish by rubbing parallel to the grain. An hour later, apply a third coat if required.

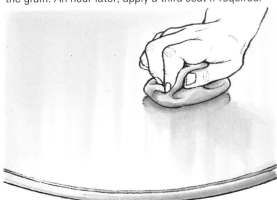

3 Buffing the surface
Leave the polish to harden, preferably overnight, then burnish the workpiece in the direction of the grain with a clean soft cloth.

Maintaining a wax finish
The color and patina of a wax finish improve with age, provided the finish receives regular care. Mop up any spilled water immediately, and dust a polished surface frequently to pick up dirt that might otherwise sink into the wax and discolor the finish. If you cannot raise a satisfactory shine by burnishing with a soft cloth, it is time to apply a fresh coat of wax. Very dowdy wax polish can be removed with mineral spirits, in preparation for refinishing.

APPLYING A WAX DRESSING
If you want to achieve the typical mellow finish of wax polish, but prefer something more hardwearing, you can apply a thin wax dressing over polyurethane varnish or cold-cure lacquer.

Dip 000-grade steel wool or an abrasive nylon pad in paste polish, and rub the finished surface using long straight strokes, parallel with the grain. Leave the wax to harden for 15 to 20 minutes, then polish it with a soft cloth.

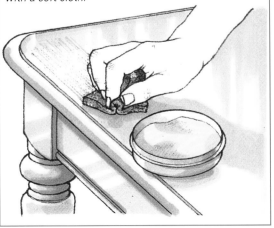

TYPES OF OIL FINISH

Some woodworkers consider oil finishes as being suitable only for hardwoods such as teak or afrormosia; this is primarily because they are associated in people's minds with the fashion for Scandinavian-style furniture and interior design. In fact, oil makes a handsome finish for any wood, especially pine, which turns a rich golden color when it is oiled.

Pine staircase finished with hardwearing gelled oil

Linseed oil

Traditional linseed oil, derived from the flax plant, is rarely used nowadays for finishing wood, mainly because it can take up to three days to dry.

Manufacturers have been able to reduce drying time to about 24 hours by heating the oil and adding driers, producing boiled linseed oil. Neither type of oil should be used as an exterior finish.

Tung oil

Also known as Chinese wood oil, tung oil is obtained from nuts grown in China and parts of South America. A tung-oil finish is resistant to water, alcohol, and acidic fruit juice, takes about 24 hours to dry, and is suitable for exterior woodwork.

Finishing oil

Commercial wood-finishing oils, based on tung oil, include synthetic resins to improve their durability. Depending on temperature and humidity, finishing oils dry in about six hours. Often referred to as teak oil or Danish oil, finishing oil is an excellent finish for any environment, and can also be used as a sealer coat for oil varnish or paint.

Non-toxic oils

Pure tung oil is non-toxic, but some manufacturers add metallic driers to it, so don't use tung oil for items that will come into contact with food unless the maker's recommendations state specifically that it is safe to do so. As an alternative, you can use ordinary olive oil or one of the special "salad-bowl" oils, sold for finishing food receptacles and chopping boards.

Gelled oil

A blend of natural oils and synthetic resin is available in a thick gel that behaves more like a soft wax polish. It is packed in tubs so the gel can be picked up on a cloth pad. Gelled oil can be applied to bare wood, and unlike other oil finishes, it can also be applied over existing finishes such as varnish and lacquer.

Preparing the surface

Since oil is a penetrating finish, it cannot be applied to a prevarnished or painted workpiece; strip a surface finish using chemical stripper. When finishing previously oiled wood, use mineral spirits to clean old wax from the surface. Prepare bare wood thoroughly (see pages 96—108), sanding it smooth with progressively finer abrasive papers.

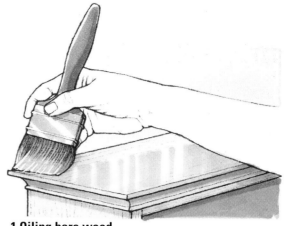

1 Oiling bare wood
Shake the container before decanting some oil into a shallow dish. Apply the first coat, using a fairly wide paintbrush to wet the surface thoroughly. Leave the oil to soak in for about 10 to 15 minutes, then make sure coverage is even by wiping excess oil from the surface with a soft cloth pad.

2 Applying additional oil with a pad
After six hours, use an abrasive nylon-fiber pad to rub oil onto the wood in the general direction of the grain. Wipe excess from the surface with a paper towel or cloth pad, then leave it to dry overnight. Apply a third coat the same way.

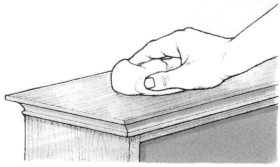

3 Modifying the finish
Leave the last coat to dry thoroughly, then burnish the surface with a cloth to raise a soft sheen.

For a smooth satin finish, dress interior woodwork with wax polish, using a clean abrasive nylon pad or fine steel wool (see page 123).

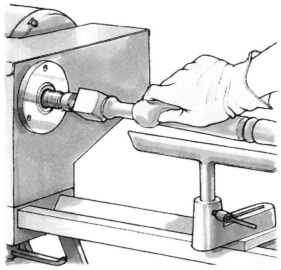

Oiling turned pieces

After sanding a turned workpiece, switch off the lathe while you rub oil onto the wood. Let it soak in for a short while, wipe off excess oil then restart the lathe and burnish by holding a cloth pad against the slowly rotating workpiece.

Applying gelled oil

Apply gelled oil to bare wood, using a soft cloth pad to rub the finish vigorously in the direction of the grain until the surface is touch-dry. Two coats are usually enough, but apply more gelled oil to a workpiece that will be subjected to heavy wear and hot dishes; allow four hours between coats. Apply gelled oil sparingly over an existing finish.

Since gelled oil dries naturally to a soft sheen, there is no need to burnish the workpiece again, but allow a full 48 hours before you put it to use.

From time to time, wipe the workpiece with a damp cloth to remove surface marks and fingerprints.

Maintaining an oiled finish

An oiled surface is very hardwearing and under normal circumstances requires nothing more than an occasional wipe with a damp cloth to maintain the finish. A faded finish can be revitalized by applying a light coat of oil, provided you remove any wax dressing first. Wipe the surface dry before oiling.

Oil exterior woodwork at regular intervals, taking care to treat all surfaces with at least one coat.

Fire precautions

As oil oxidizes it generates heat, which can cause oil-soaked rags to burst into flames. Spread out used rags to dry thoroughly outside, or soak them in a bucket of water overnight before disposing of them.

FAULTS AND REMEDIES

Oiling wood is so easy that success is practically guaranteed, provided you have prepared the work-piece adequately and you don't leave the oil to become sticky.

Sticky surface

If you leave excess oil on the surface for longer than about an hour, it thickens and becomes sticky.
Don't attempt to wipe off oil if it reaches this stage. Instead, use an abrasive nylon pad to apply a light dressing of fresh oil to wet the surface again, then wipe with a cloth pad or paper towel.

White rings

Hot plates or dishes may leave white rings on an oiled surface.
These blemishes are usually temporary and disappear of their own accord within a short time.